ORGANIZATION HACKS

Over 350 Simple Solutions to Organize Your Home IN NO TIME!

CARRIE HIGGINS

Creator of MakingLemonadeBlog.com

Adams Media

New York   London   Toronto   Sydney   New Delhi

Adams Media
An Imprint of Simon & Schuster, Inc.
57 Littlefield Street
Avon, Massachusetts 02322

First Adams Media trade paperback edition DECEMBER 2017

ADAMS MEDIA and colophon are trademarks of Simon and Schuster.

For information about special discounts for bulk purchases, please contact Simon & Schuster Special Sales at 1-866-506-1949 or business@simonandschuster.com.

The Simon & Schuster Speakers Bureau can bring authors to your live event. For more information or to book an event contact the Simon & Schuster Speakers Bureau at 1-866-248-3049 or visit our website at www.simonspeakers.com.

Interior design by Erin Alexander and Colleen Cunningham
Interior illustrations by Nicola DosSantos

Manufactured in the United States of America

10 9 8 7 6 5 4 3 2 1

Library of Congress Cataloging-in-Publication Data has been applied for.

ISBN 978-1-5072-0333-0
ISBN 978-1-5072-0334-7 (ebook)

For my tribe,
Abby, Ben, and Casey...
for more reasons than could ever fit on this page.

ACKNOWLEDGMENTS

So much gratitude, so little space! First, thank you to those who've both inspired and believed in me, including my parents, friends, and family. Heaps of thanks to those who shared their favorite hacks whether it was while brainstorming around the kitchen table or in general being an organization rockstar (Nicky, Rachel, and Kelli I'm looking at you). Several hacks in this book came from brilliant friends who blog, specifically Diane of InMyOwnStyle.com, Jocie from OneProjectCloser.com/TheBetter Half, and Sandra of Sawdust Girl.com. In addition, Wagner SprayTech generously provided a spray tent and home decor sprayer to facilitate easy painting of several larger projects. Many thanks to Rebecca Tarr Thomas, Zander Hatch, and the team at Adams Media for endless patience and support helping to turn this book into a reality. To the *Making Lemonade* blog readers and community, thanks for allowing me to do what I love and call it a job; your incredible support is both humbling and deeply appreciated.

This book would not have been possible without the support of my incredible husband Casey who pitched in and cheered me on without complaint. I thank my lucky stars each day for you. To my amazing children, Abby and Ben, who exuded excitement and offered help, whether in the form of dance parties, snuggles, or being an "assistant" while I worked on projects: I'm deeply thankful for you and your willingness to embrace challenges. I did this for you and hope I made you proud.

CONTENTS

INTRODUCTION

. . . .

Imagine your perfect life: You have more time for the things you love. You have a little extra money in your pocket. There's less stress in your life. There isn't nearly as much chaos swirling around you as there seems to be now. While you might not achieve perfection, the organization hacks in this book can help make all these wishes come true. You'll save time by quickly finding any item you need; be more efficient when deciding what to wear each day; spend less money replacing lost or improperly stored items; and enjoy a calmer, more peaceful environment once you ditch the clutter and chaos.

Throughout this book, you will find three types of hacks: the short hack, the DIY project, and the list. The short hacks in each chapter are simple ideas that quickly solve a problem. One or two of these hacks alone may not do much, but as you implement more of these and begin getting into an organized mindset, the benefits will quickly add up. The DIY projects are more in depth than the hacks and can be tweaked to fit different rooms and spaces. Each DIY project should be able to be completed in under three hours, with most of them taking far less time. Finally, the lists shine a spotlight on several ways to hack a featured item or several ways to tackle a specific problem. Use these lists to find the tip that works best for you, to brainstorm the best way to execute an organization hack, or to come up with your own unique use for handy items.

Each person is different, which means there's not a "one-size-fits-all" method of organizing. To that end, you may notice several hacks to choose from that are focused on one common organization problem. Sometimes you want a quick fix; other times you don't mind taking on a larger DIY project. Choose the one that best fits your schedule, habits, and routine. Combined, this format of short hacks, DIY projects, and lists that are tailored specifically to each area of your home provides one powerhouse of an organization plan!

HOW TO GET STARTED

Laying the groundwork for organizing is almost as important as the actual projects. Before you begin, ensure success by taking a moment to set your organizing vision, review the list of basic organizing necessities, and learn the Ten Commandments of Organizing. Each one is important, but together they create a framework that will help you set yourself up for continued success.

The first thing you want to do is to consider the end goal. Take a moment and jot down *why* you want to get organized. What does an organized home look like to you? What does it feel like? What will happen when you get organized? Considering these questions is important; these reasons will give you a clear goal to work toward and a reminder of the end goal when you're in the thick of it. Organization comes from having a clear and executable plan. Once you've laid out your goals, you're ready to begin to gather supplies.

General Organizing Supplies

Now that you're in the right mindset to get organized, let's get everything you need to be successful. As a rule, it's best to sort first and determine your needs before buying any new products for organizing. However, there are a few basic supplies that you should have on hand before you begin, including:

- ❏ Camera or smartphone for taking photos of important papers and/or kids' art
- ❏ Cleaning wipes
- ❏ Cordless drill
- ❏ Set of general purpose drill and driver bits
- ❏ Hammer
- ❏ Hot glue gun
- ❏ 1 package of 50 hot glue sticks
- ❏ Labels
- ❏ Label maker with label tape
- ❏ Level
- ❏ Measuring tape
- ❏ Pencil
- ❏ 1 box each of snack-, sandwich-, quart-, and gallon-sized plastic zip-top bags
- ❏ 1 (1.88" × 60") roll of painter's tape
- ❏ Post-it notes
- ❏ Ruler
- ❏ Scissors
- ❏ 1 package (1") screws
- ❏ 1 package (2") screws
- ❏ 1 black Sharpie marker
- ❏ Stud finder
- ❏ 1 box kitchen-sized white trash bags

Place them in a basket or caddy that you can carry from room to room so they're always within reach when needed. Store it in the same place at the end of each organizing session so that you can quickly find it each time you're ready to start again. Those basic supplies and the hacks in this book are pretty much all you need to create an organization system that works for you!

The Ten Commandments of Organizing

There are a few basic principles—you may even want to call them "commandments"—you need to know before jumping into organizing your home. Read them, do them, *live them*. Consider photocopying this information and pinning it to a bulletin board. Each time you start to organize, reread it until it sinks in. Once these commandments become habits, getting (and more important, *staying*) organized will become part of your daily routine. That not only saves time but also energy, stress, and money!

Do Not Organize Junk

In other words, do a thorough decluttering and purge before you begin so you don't waste energy and space organizing items you don't need, use, or love. When decluttering a space, first take everything out. Then clean the space with a thorough dusting, scrubbing, or polishing. Instead of trying to decide what you should get rid of, frame the question as "What should I keep?" Touch each item, and put back only what you need and love. Have a system in place for getting rid of the rest such as a donation bin or trash bag, and dispose of them as soon as possible.

Start with Easier Spaces First to Gain Momentum

Your closet is a great place to start because it's easy to figure out what doesn't fit or look good anymore. Tackle the time-consuming or emotional areas like photographs later, after you've worked up confidence and experienced how great it feels when you conquer the small "wins"!

Keep Flat Surfaces Clear

Keeping flat surfaces clear is visually appealing and will make everything appear neater and more organized. Flat surfaces such as tables, desks, and countertops occupy a large horizontal area so they look (and feel) airy and calm when they are clutter-free. Find ways to stow most of your items out of sight, and keep those flat surfaces as clear as possible to instantly create the appearance of organization.

Gather and Sort First, Then Organize

Resist the urge to buy organizing supplies until you know exactly how much of an item you are storing, and where. When possible, use what you have on hand to organize first, and then purchase additional supplies only if needed.

Make It Attractive

If you do purchase bins and baskets, keep them neutral and classic so they fit with any decor, are easy to find, and allow you to add more if needed. When you hack something, you should paint, decorate, or arrange it in a way that it makes you happy when you see it. Make storage do double duty; for example, that beautiful basket on the shelf can be decorative, but it also can be used to stash unused remotes.

Give Everything a Home

The common phrase "a place for everything, and everything in its place" is a simple yet brilliant mantra for keeping your home organized. One of the biggest reasons for clutter is not knowing where to put something. Once you designate a spot for an item (or category of items), it has a home. This will help you and your family to make a habit of putting it away properly.

Group All the Like Items in Your Home Together

As you organize, first consolidate *everything* in each category so you can see how much you have, and then store those items together. For example, if you've stashed batteries all over your home, gather them up and keep them in one accessible spot instead. Now you know exactly what you have and where to find it each time you need it.

Finish Each Task

Complete each organizing project or task fully before moving on to the next one. Block enough time for cleanup, as that usually takes quite a bit of effort. Be realistic in your expectations or else you'll burn out before you really begin.

Do What Works Best for You

Each person organizes differently. There's no "one-size-fits-all" method that can be applied to every family and situation. Discover the solutions that best work for *your* family and situation. In many cases, there are several hacks in this book that cover a single organization challenge; choose the one that works best for you and rock it.

Make Organizing a Part of Your Daily Routine
In addition to tackling the larger projects, devote a few minutes each day to organizing and decluttering. Organizing is not "one and done." This is a continual process—make it part of your daily habits and reap the rewards!

Jump Right In

Now that you're properly prepared, the best advice I can give you is to just start. Blast the tunes, listen to a podcast or audiobook, light some candles, and make organizing both fun and productive. Not sure where to begin? Go chapter by chapter through the book until you are done, or turn to the page that most speaks to you and your needs. We've designed this book so you can jump in on any page and just get started. I suggest you start with the area that you can knock out the quickest; choose the area that once it's done will continue to motivate you the most. As you incorporate these systems and hacks into your routine, continually evaluate if they are working for you. Are you keeping up with the system? Did it solve your problem? If not, tweak it until it works.

If you commit to one hack a day, at the end of the year you'll be fully organized. That sounds pretty great, right? Whether you picked up this book to become better organized or because life feels out of control and you need help, my hope is you are able to implement these ideas, which in turn will bring you peace, clarity, and extra time to do more of what you love.

01

Do you ever feel like you have nothing to wear or are mentally exhausted from trying to sleep amidst a bedside table filled with clutter? The clever hacks in this chapter ensure you can reach right into your closet and immediately find the perfect piece, locate an accessory to complement any outfit, and rest easily with your bedroom tidily organized. You'll also learn how to carve out storage in underutilized areas and get tips on how to make the most of the space you already have.

BEDROOMS AND CLOSETS

CLOSETS

· · · · · · · · · · · ·

After you take a piece of clothing off the hanger, move that hanger to a dedicated "empty hanger" spot in your closet. With no more stray hangers hogging up valuable closet space, you'll immediately be able to find a new one when placing clothes back inside.

———

Items such as tank tops, V-necks, and dresses can easily slide off regular hangers. Make your own nonslip hangers by wrapping a pipe cleaner around the top ends of the hanger. The pipe cleaners act as grippers, the clothes stay where they belong, and you've spent mere pennies on this clever solution.

———

After you declutter your clothing and get rid of anything you don't love, hang the clothes you are keeping back up, but with the hanger facing backward. Then as you wear an item, place it back in the closet with the hanger facing the correct way. Around every three months or at the time you traditionally switch clothes for the season, evaluate the items with backward-facing hangers. With this method you can instantly see what you didn't wear and you feel good getting rid of it.

You can double your closet space by slipping the large hole of a soda can tab through the hook of a clothes hanger, and then using the bottom hole to hang another hanger. You'll have instant double hangers! Now you can hang twice as many items in one space.

———

Hang a tote bag in the closet and use it to corral items for the dry cleaner or tailor. A second tote bag can serve as a place to hold items to donate (just don't mix up the two!).

———

Handbags should be stored with filler inside so they maintain their shape. Stuff tissue paper in gallon-sized resealable bags and place inside the purse. Now, it's a cinch to pull out the filler when you are using the bag and replace when finished.

———

Stuff larger handbags with smaller ones. This method makes it harder to see your individual bags, but the plus side is it saves lots of closet space as well as helps the bags keep their shape.

———

Arrange the hanging clothing in your closet by type (bottoms, short sleeves, long sleeves, jackets, etc.) and then by color. This not only makes them visually appealing but easier to find.

SCARF ORGANIZER FROM SHOWER CURTAIN RINGS

Scarves are a staple in many closets, and they tend to overtake the space unless properly stored. This quick scarf organizer can be made for just a few dollars and will make hanging and storing your scarves a breeze. It can also be used for belts and ties, so it's multifunctional.

WHAT YOU'LL NEED

12 plastic shower curtain rings

Ruler

Scissors

1 (¾" × 180") roll mini duct tape

Sturdy wooden hanger

INSTRUCTIONS

1. Open your package of shower curtain rings and place on a table in three rows of four rings.

2. Measure and cut twenty-one 4" strips of mini duct tape.

3. Using a strip of mini duct tape, attach the first ring to the second. It's easiest to wrap it around the side of the first ring so the tape grips, then continue to wrap it around the adjoining side of the second ring. Continue until you have three rows of four attached rings.

4. Attach the bottom of the first row to the top of the second row using the duct tape wrapping technique in step two. Next, attach the bottom of the second row to the top of the last row.

5. Now that all the rings are joined, attach the entire piece onto the hanger by wrapping a piece of duct tape around the top of the first ring and the bottom of the hanger. Repeat with the remaining top row of rings until all four rings are joined with the hanger, and thread your scarves through the rings.

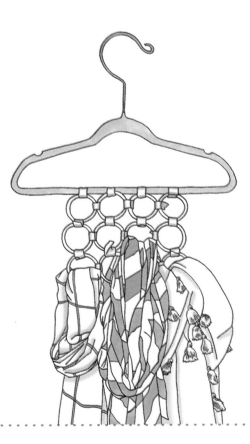

If you have an odd nook or cranny in your closet, put it to work by using a tension rod in that space and drape belts and scarves over it.

––––––

Shoe care supplies such as shoe polish and boot spray can get messy. Dedicate a plastic shoe box for these supplies in the closet so they don't accidentally stain clothing but are always within reach when you need a quick buff or polish.

––––––

If you have wooden shelves in your closet, affix a towel rod with S-hooks or an open-ended toilet roll holder underneath as a way to hang bags, scarves, and jewelry. That leaves the shelves free for other items and also uses the formerly wasted space below.

––––––

Typically reserved for the kitchen, three-tier hanging baskets are great for storing hats, gloves, and other easily lost items. They also work well to utilize horizontal space.

––––––

Invest in replacing old wire hangers with slim velvet-lined or wooden ones. They protect your clothes better and will make your entire closet look cohesive and upscale.

Plastic six-pack soda can rings (the type that holds the cans together and usually get recycled) can serve as an impromptu scarf holder. Place the hook of a hanger through one of the small holes on the short side and let it hang. Loop scarves through the larger holes and voilà, quick and packable storage for your scarves.

———

Put a bookcase along that blank wall in your closet. It will allow for more clothing or shoe storage and it's way cheaper than custom shelves.

———

Fill an empty closet wall with various-sized hooks. Shaker-style peg hooks can hold caps and hats (and even shoes, if placed near the floor). Use large hooks for towels or robes, and use smaller hooks for scarves, handbags, and jewelry.

———

Leave your closet floors free of shoes and other items to make vacuuming easier and clutter less likely to sprout like weeds. Consistent vacuuming helps keep your closets pest-free, and it's much easier to convince yourself to do it when nothing stands in your way.

10 CLEVER WAYS TO ORGANIZE JEWELRY

Bracelets, necklaces, rings, and earrings each have unique characteristics that make organizing them a challenge. Thankfully, you can pick and choose the hacks from this list that best fit your needs and style. The best part is they look great when grouped together!

1. Stack bracelets in a pretty bowl on your dresser.

2. Screw cup hooks into the wall or to a board that you've painted with a favorite color, and use to hang your necklaces.

3. A wide vase makes jewelry stand out when draped over the vase's neck and laid down the front. It's a beautiful way to combine decor and storage right out in the open.

4. Finger towel holders, usually reserved for bathrooms, have two straight rods sticking out from either side, which makes them perfect for hanging necklaces or bracelets.

5. The small indentations in ice cube trays make them especially suitable for sorting jewelry such as rings and earrings, and can be stacked on top of one another for layers of storage.

6. Muffin tins are the perfect size for storing rolled-up necklaces, bracelets, or earrings.

7. Large statement necklaces fit well in the pockets of a clear over-the-door shoe pocket organizer, and they'll be protected from dust if you push the top of the pockets closed.

8. Wedge-shaped makeup sponges can be squeezed to fit inside rings. Their soft texture protects the ring, and the flat bottom is ideal for holding them in place. Place the secured rings inside a box, and you have a new DIY ring holder.

9. Use a staple gun to attach chicken wire, available at many craft stores, across the back of an open picture frame. Hang it on the wall and use it to organize your earrings.

10. Stack bracelets around empty glass soda bottles and they'll become a tower of beauty!

Boots should be stored the same way they are worn, straight up and filled, so they don't lose shape. Cut inexpensive pool noodles to fit in the calf/leg area of the boot to create your own boot stocks. No more wrinkled boots flopping over on the floor, which is especially important during the summer storage months.

If you don't have pool noodles on hand, use rolled-up magazines inside the boots instead. This is the same idea as the noodles, but it costs nothing to implement.

Arrange shoes by use, such as dressy, casual, sporty, flip-flops, and boots. This way it's much easier to find the type of shoe you need quickly, and they fit together better as well.

Fit more shoes onto shelves by alternating the direction of each shoe in a pair. For example, place one heel forward and the toe of its mate forward, so they are standing heel to toe.

Use clear boxes to store shoes. This way, you keep them dust-free but can still view contents easily. Better yet, store them in plastic drawers so you can simply pull out the drawer instead of shuffling boxes to get the pair you want.

Low open shelving is the perfect place to store shoes. The shelves should be placed far enough off the ground so that it is easy to vacuum underneath but low enough that they fit below hanging clothing. Then add your shoes. They'll be easy to see and grab as needed.

When folding shirts to store in drawers, fold and stack them sideways like books on a shelf as opposed to laying them on top of one another. This makes them easier to see, and you can grab the one you need without digging through the pile and potentially unfolding all your hard work.

If your bedroom is small, place your dresser in a closet. Then you can use the clothing hanger rod to hang short items above it. This gives you both hanging and folded storage options.

NO-SEW CLOTHING PROTECTION COVER

Plastic dry cleaning bags are not only unattractive in your closet but may trap moisture that damages clothing. They can also be a hazard for small children. Fix that by replacing them with easy sew-free clothing covers that protect off-season clothes while beautifying your closet at the same time.

WHAT YOU'LL NEED

1 large pillowcase

Iron

Sturdy wooden hanger

Ruler

Thin-tipped marker

Scissors

1 (1.25-ounce) tube Liquid Stitch Permanent Adhesive

12" (¼"-width) single-faced ribbon

INSTRUCTIONS

1. Wash, dry, and iron the pillowcase. Arrange so that the opening is at the bottom of your workspace and the edge with the fold is at the top.

2. Create the opening for the hanger. First, determine the center of the top edge where your hanger will poke through and use your ruler to measure about 2" out from the center on each

side, a total of about 4" across the top. Draw a line with the thin-tipped marker so you'll know where to cut.

3. At both ends of this line, make a ¼" cut using scissors through both layers of the pillowcase perpendicular to the line. Insert scissors into either of these holes and cut through the line you drew across the top. Now, apply a thin line of Liquid Stitch along the inside of one edge and fold down toward the inside to create a seam. Repeat with the other side and let dry according to the package directions.

4. Finally, use Liquid Stitch to glue four sections of ribbon around the opening for a streamlined look and let dry according to package directions. Once dry, place your clothing on the hanger and poke the hanger through the slit at the top of the pillowcase. Your clothing is now attractively protected.

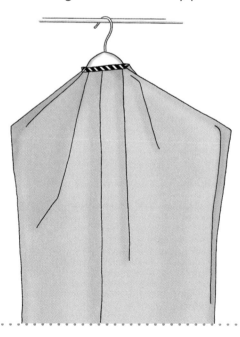

DRESSERS, DRAWERS, AND OTHER BEDROOM STORAGE

· ·

Single socks are a notorious adversary of laundry day. Set out a small "lost sock bin" to toss them inside when you find a straggler. Then once a month or so, dump them out and match them up.

———

Make your own sock dividers by using the cardboard inserts that separate bottles inside twenty-four-packs of beer. Cut these inserts in half the long way. Then place them in drawers and tuck socks and rolled underwear into the openings.

———

Bras should be stored the same way they are displayed in high-end lingerie shops: laid flat, with the hooks clasped behind. This way they maintain their shape and there's less wear and tear on delicate pieces.

JEWELRY FRAME

The brilliance of this hack is you can tailor it to fit not only your needs but your style as well. You can use a beautiful vintage frame or run to the store and buy one that's brand spankin' new (just make sure it's made of wood to make stapling easier). In under thirty minutes you'll have an easy way to display your jewelry, bows, and hair clips.

WHAT YOU'LL NEED

2 hot glue sticks

Hot glue gun

Ruler

Scissors

4' (1"-width) grosgrain ribbon

1 (11" × 14") wooden frame with hanging hardware

Staple gun with staples

Pencil

Hammer

1 (1½") nail

INSTRUCTIONS

1. Insert a hot glue stick into the hot glue gun and plug it in so it heats up, approximately five minutes. Use the ruler and scissors to measure and cut the ribbons into four 10" strips.

2. Flip the frame so the back side is facing up with the shorter sides at the top and bottom of your workspace. Evenly space the ribbon horizontally across the back of the frame. If you wish to use the frame to store earrings, you'll need at least one row of lace ribbon.

3. Working top to bottom, use the hot glue gun to glue one side of each ribbon to the back using the eraser end of the pencil to apply pressure on top of the ribbon so it adheres to the frame. Once dry (about two minutes), pull the ribbon tight enough across the opening that it won't warp but not so tight it loses shape, and then glue this side in the same manner. Repeat for all four pieces of ribbon.

4. Now that the ribbon is laid out and lightly attached where you want it, starting at the top, staple one side of each ribbon into the wood using the staple gun. If your ribbon is wide, it might take two staples to cover the entire width of the ribbon. Once attached, staple the other end into the frame. Work your way down until all the ribbons are attached tightly across.

5. Hang your jewelry frame on the wall using your hammer and nail and load up with your jewelry or hair bows.

PERSONALIZED JEWELRY AND KEY HOLDER

Using the letter of your first or last initial makes this jewelry or key holder personalized and fun. While we are going to use paint in this tutorial, you can get creative by covering the letter in fabric, washi tape, or yarn. There are so many ways you can style it up to make it your own!

WHAT YOU'LL NEED

Newspaper

*Large wooden letter with notch in back for hanging
(mine was 21" × 14")*

1 (2-ounce) bottle craft paint

1 (½") paintbrush

10 adhesive hooks, small and clear

INSTRUCTIONS

1. Lay down several sheets of newspaper to protect your workspace.

2. Paint the front and sides of the letter until the wood grain no longer shows through (about three coats of paint), letting each coat dry for approximately twenty minutes before applying the next. Let dry fully for about twenty-four hours.

3. Once the letter is dry, add your hooks. Lay them out first on the front of the letter so you know where you would like them, then once they are in the correct spot peel and stick the adhesive back and apply pressure to adhere. Let the adhesive-backed hooks cure for twenty-four hours.

4. Once the adhesive hooks are set, hang it on the wall and start adding your jewelry or keys. Don't be surprised if friends start asking you to make this stylish storage solution for them as well!

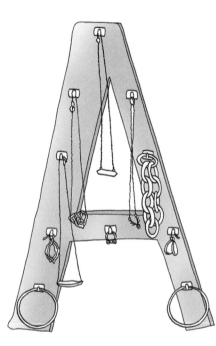

If you have a collection you need to keep out of the way or have little closet space, install a shelf around the perimeter of your room toward the ceiling. You can tuck your collectables there so they become decor. Or you can use the shelves to store shoes, books, or handbags you don't use often.

No closet at all? A sturdy shelf with a hanger rod installed underneath is a perfect place to hang clothes. This works great in corners because it uses space that's typically wasted.

For top secret hidden storage, use a full-length framed mirror and install long hinges along one of the sides. Attach the hinges to the wall, and swing it open to reveal hidden storage behind it. You can install small cup hooks directly into the wall behind the mirror and use them to store jewelry, making it easy to check out your outfit in the morning, and then quickly grab matching accessories behind it.

10 WAYS TO USE HANGING SHOE POCKET ORGANIZERS

Over-the-door shoe pockets aren't just for footwear! They come in several materials, including clear plastic for when you want to see what's inside and cloth for when you don't. With all those gorgeous pockets, and the ability to fit them in such a slim and underutilized area, shoe pockets are an organizing superstar. Here's how to manage their star power:

1. Place them on the inside of your utility closet and fill with cleaning supplies such as cleaning sprays, dusters, rags, and latex gloves.

2. They make excellent art supply organizers—markers, colored pencils, brushes, and more, all lined up and ready to use.

3. Using clear pockets, create a jewelry organizer on the back of a closet or door. Large pockets are best suited for bulky jewelry such as statement necklaces and bracelets.

4. Attach clear shoe pockets to the wall of your garage by hanging with hooks or screws in the grommets, and fill with small hardware and miscellaneous items grouped together by category such as screws, cable ties, and nails sorted by type. This makes finding correctly sized hardware a breeze.

5. Roll scarves and tuck them into pockets. This is especially great for thin scarves that would otherwise easily snag.

6. Stash winter items such as hats, gloves, and thick socks into the pockets that hang inside the door of your coat closet. When summer arrives, switch them out for sunscreen, sun hats, and sunglasses.

7. For any parents reading this, small toys and stuffed animals will find a happy home in shoe pockets when used in kids' rooms.

8. Hair ties, headbands, bows, and bobby pins fit neatly inside over-the-door pockets. They will be easily visible if you use clear pockets.

9. As long as the spices are bagged or bottled, you can use clear shoe pockets on the back of a pantry door. This makes them easy to find because you can see what you need instantly.

10. Crafters will find they can use the pockets for washi tape, skeins of yarn, or a variety of other essential crafting items.

BEDS AND NIGHTSTANDS

Prepare your bedroom as a haven for sleep and relaxation by keeping away clutter such as exercise equipment or a television. If you must keep them in the bedroom, house the TV in an armoire that can be closed when not in use or the treadmill behind a folding screen. Doing so keeps them from being dust collectors and also eliminates needless visual clutter.

Most people read only one book at a time, so reduce nightstand clutter by keeping just that one book on top. Store the rest in a bookcase or inside nightstand drawers so that the avalanche of books that used to occupy the top will be a distant memory.

Place a storage bench at the end of your bed to store blankets and extra pillows. It also serves as a good place to sit while getting dressed or putting on shoes.

Luggage racks come in handy if you have guests often, but you can also repurpose them as nightstands (and extra storage) by placing a hard-sided vintage suitcase or large tray on top. Store items in the suitcase, and top with a pretty vase or a few books.

Stack vintage suitcases on top of one another with the smallest on top and use as a nightstand. You can even paint them all so they look cohesive and use them for extra storage.

———

Instead of throwing your pajamas over a chair every morning, fold them and place under your pillow instead. Your bedroom will look neater and you'll always know where to find your pj's.

———

Color-code your sheet sets by size so that all the king sheets are the same color, all queens another, etc. This way you can instantly pull out the correct-sized sheets without having to check the tags. Buy two sets of sheets for each mattress in your home, one to keep on the bed and one in the linen closet, to make sure you have enough on hand.

———

A time-saving trick on laundry day is to wash your sheets and then place them right back on the bed after drying so you can skip folding. It's still a good idea to have an extra sheet set per mattress just in case, but this "lazy" trick is a favorite in our home on laundry day.

HOW TO PROPERLY FOLD
A FITTED SHEET

There seem to be polarizing opinions on how to fold a fitted sheet. You have your folders and you have your ballers. The truth is, there really is only one way to fold a fitted sheet so that it lays flat. Once you learn these simple steps you'll never go back. Folding them properly takes about one minute tops and ensures your linens are neat, less wrinkled, and easy to take out one at a time when needed.

WHAT YOU'LL NEED

Fitted sheet

Flat surface (such as a bed)

INSTRUCTIONS

1. While standing up, hold the sheet and find the two corners of the sheet on the long side. Place your hands as deep inside the elastic corners as they'll go.

2. Bring your hands together as if you're performing a gigantic clap until both palms are touching through the sheet.

3. Push one corner inside the other and gently shake until they lay flat.

4. Lay the sheet flat on the bed with the elastic corners toward the top, and then tuck the opposite two corners together. You now have a rectangle on the bed, folded in half with the elastic corners toward the top, tucked inside themselves, and lying flat.

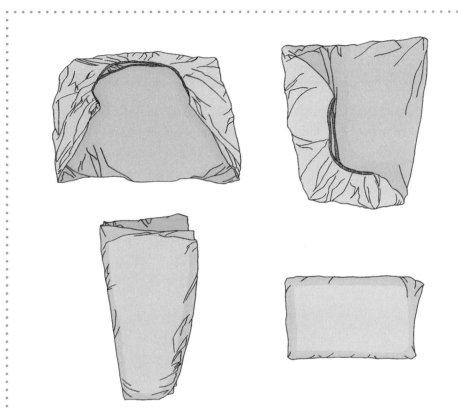

5. Swipe your hands across the sheet to push out any wrinkles and make sure it's flat, then fold up the bottom half to meet the top.

6. Wipe any wrinkles out again, and this time, fold in half sideways across the length. Then fold in half sideways one more time.

7. Finally, fold up from the bottom and you'll have a perfectly flat and folded fitted sheet. Match it with the top sheet and put everything, including any additional pillowcases, inside the matching pillowcase so your entire sheet set is together and ready to use.

BEDSIDE STORAGE POCKETS

This project is particularly handy when space is tight (such as in a dorm room) or for those who don't have a nightstand. The pockets provide ample room for common bedside needs such as books, water bottles, and eyeglasses. Plus, the pockets can be adjusted depending on the height of the bed, making them a versatile solution for bedroom storage.

WHAT YOU'LL NEED

Measuring tape

Scissors

Hanging (24-pocket) shoe organizer

INSTRUCTIONS

1. Determine how many pockets will fit hanging between the mattress or box spring and the floor. Most beds can accommodate one row of pockets. If the bed is on risers, you might be able to fit more rows. You will also need to keep an extra row of pockets attached to tuck under the mattress. So, at minimum, you'll need two rows of shoe pockets. These measurements will be your guide for cutting the shoe pocket organizer.

2. Keeping your measurements in mind, use the scissors to cut straight across the width along the backing area (make sure not to cut through the actual pockets) until you have two or three rows of pockets, depending on the height of your bed.

3. Tuck one row of pockets under the mattress and let the rest hang down to the floor.

4. Repeat with the remaining pockets to double or even triple your storage.

5. Now, fill with necessities: water bottles, books, magazines, lip balm, reading glasses, and more.

Storage under the bed is perfect for seasonal items that you know you'll use eventually but you don't need every day. It's also a great place for larger items due to the square footage available under your bed. No matter what you place under your bed, it's a good idea to keep it in a flat plastic bin or bag so it doesn't fall victim to dust bunnies.

———

Bed risers are an inexpensive way to add lots of storage space by allowing you to use the area under the bed. You can buy them, or you can make your own by using thick, evenly sized wooden blocks placed under each leg of the bed. If you go the DIY route, make sure the blocks have an indent in the top to fit the width of the bed leg so they stay in place.

———

Make a divided storage drawer that fits in the space under your bed using a lightweight bookcase. To create this handy roll-away storage, attach casters to the four corners on the back of a bookcase and two handles on the long side, lay the bookcase on its back, and roll it under the bed.

02

Kitchens and eating spaces are the heart of the home, but with so many utensils and supplies it's an area that can easily get out of control. These tips will help you organize everything from spatulas to food so you can spend more time with family and less time wondering just where you put that jar of paprika. The hacks in this chapter will help you hide everyday tools yet still put them within your reach. You will also find tips for keeping your food fresh and cleverly stored for easy access. Whether you have a formal dining room or an eat-in kitchen, you'll find you have more than enough space when every inch is used in a beautiful and meaningful way.

KITCHEN AND DINING

COUNTERTOPS

First things first: divide and organize your kitchen into zones according to their function, such as baking, food prep, and cleaning. Doing so will put everything you need for that task within reach, saving you both time and space.

For items you need to keep on the countertops, arrange them grouped on trays for increased productivity and visual appeal. It looks better and is functional as well.

Create a coffee station by gathering all your coffee supplies in one area and arranging on a tray next to your machine. No more stumbling around bleary-eyed in the morning trying to get your caffeine fix!

Turn an extra drawer into a tea storage and preparation area. Use drawer dividers (or a utensil holder) sized to fit tea bags to showcase various types of tea. Add in pretty strainers, tea bag holders, or other tea making accessories.

Make your mugs part of your decor. Attach small cup hooks evenly spaced under cabinets and hang mugs from their handles. They'll be ready to use when needed and double as decoration.

———

Utensil storage doesn't have to be boring. Use a small garden urn, vintage pitcher, or wide mouthed vase to hold your utensils for a twist on a classic storage idea. You can also check out the Metal Can to Faux Bois Utensil Holder project later in this chapter to make your own utensil canister from a metal can.

———

Attach a magnetic knife holder to your backsplash in the food prep area as a practical and stylish way to keep hands safe and knives sharp. They'll also be within reach every time you need to chop something.

———

Attach a knife sharpener to the side of your knife block so it's always handy.

CUSTOM DRAWER DIVIDERS

Drawer dividers aren't just for utensils any more. The good news is you don't need to fork over a lot of cash to buy them. Instead, you can create these drawer dividers yourself. As a result, you'll have a customized system for every drawer in your home. Since the dimensions of the drawers will vary as much as your needs, use this tutorial as a framework for making the dividers and then plug in the exact measurements.

WHAT YOU'LL NEED

2 hot glue sticks

Hot glue gun

Ruler

1 kitchen drawer (I used one measuring 20" × 10½" × 3" inside)

Pencil

1 sheet of paper

1 (20" × 30" × ³/₁₆") foam core board

1 (12" × 18") cutting mat

X-Acto knife

INSTRUCTIONS

1. Insert a hot glue stick into the hot glue gun and plug it in so it heats up, approximately five minutes. Then, using your ruler, measure the length (L"), the width (W"), and the height (H") of the interior of your drawer and write them down on a piece of paper.

2. Placing the foam board horizontally on the cutting mat, use the ruler to measure H" down from the top edge (mine was 3" height) and draw a line horizontally across the entire foam board at that mark with your pencil. Using the ruler as a straightedge, cut along that line with your X-Acto knife all the way across the foam board. Repeat this until you have cut six foam strips.

3. Use your ruler to measure L" down one of your foam strips and mark that spot with your pencil. Cut across the strip at this mark with your X-Acto knife, using your ruler to ensure a straight line. Repeat this process so you have two foam strips that are H" × L". Place these strips along the sides of the drawer.

4. Take another long foam strip and use your ruler to measure W" along it. Mark a spot slightly inside that length so the strip will fit between the two longer strips when you put it in the drawer. Cut along the line with your X-Acto knife, using your ruler to ensure a straight line. Repeat this process so you have two foam strips that are just slightly smaller than the width of the drawer so they fit snugly against the two previous strips.

5. Take the strips out of the drawer and arrange the four pieces into a rectangular box. Take one of the shorter pieces and use the hot glue gun to place a thin line of glue along the small edge. Quickly attach one of the long pieces and press firmly together for about one minute, and let dry an additional minute. Repeat until all four sides are attached together to make the outer frame of your divider. Place this frame in the drawer as a guide for the rest of the pieces.

6. Take another foam strip and use the ruler and pencil to measure and mark slightly less than L". Using the ruler as a straight-edge, cut the strip straight across at this mark with your X-Acto knife. Repeat this until you have two foam strips for your vertical dividers.

7. Place these vertical dividers inside the drawer and space them evenly within the frame. Use your pencil to mark these spots on the frame then take the vertical dividers out.

8. Use the hot glue gun to place a thin line of glue along the edges of the dividers, one piece at a time, and quickly insert them back into the frame at the marked spots. Let these dry for two minutes before you go on to the next step.

9. Now you'll create the horizontal part of the dividers. Measure the distance from the left edge of the leftmost vertical divider to the right edge of the drawer frame and write it down on your piece of paper. Do the same with the other piece of foam board on the right: Measure edge to edge and notate. Then measure the distance for the middle space: Measure from the right edge of the left piece to the left edge of the right and write it down.

10. Take the final foam strip and measure out the three distances you just wrote down with the ruler, marking each spot with your pencil. Using the ruler as a straightedge, cut across the strip with your X-Acto knife at each mark.

11. Place these dividers horizontally in the frame, one in each row, approximately midway up the drawer or whichever configuration best fits your utensils. Use your pencil to mark these spots with a small line then take the horizontal dividers out. Use the hot glue gun to place a thin line of glue along the edges and quickly insert them back into the frame at the marked spots. Let these dry for two minutes. Once dry, load up with your utensils and marvel at your newly organized drawer!

CABINETS, DRAWERS, AND ISLANDS

Paint the inside door of a cabinet with chalkboard paint. Use it to jot down grocery lists, reminders, and handy measurement conversions.

Using mounting strips, attach a sheet of cork to the inside of a cabinet door and use pushpins to tack up recipes, labels, or notes.

You can screw small cup hooks inside a cabinet door to hang measuring spoons or cups, making sure it fits when the door is closed. Do this in the cabinets near your food prep or baking area to increase efficiency.

Wire pot lid racks can also be used to store bakeware such as cookie sheets and casserole dishes. Place them along the bottom of a cabinet with your bakeware placed on its side. This makes it much easier for you to take exactly what you need without having to continually re-arrange everything.

Keep frying pans and griddles in great shape and scratch-free by placing cut-to-size cardboard in between each item when storing. Non-stick cookware is especially easy to scratch so this trick will keep them looking like new.

———

Use a vertical paper sorter to store cutting boards. This makes it a cinch to find the right size without having to dig through a pile of boards.

———

Spear old wine corks on the ends of sharp utensils. This works great with kabob skewers and barbecue forks to ensure you won't injure yourself when reaching for them.

———

If cleaning products clutter your under-sink area, mount a café-sized curtain rod a quarter of the way down and use it to hang your spray cleaners by the trigger handle. Now you have room for baskets underneath to organize the rest.

CHALKBOARD WALL

Chalkboard walls can be used in many ways: as a meal planner, a family calendar, doodle space, memo board, quote wall, or to-do list. Plus they look great, so it's a win-win situation all around. Put this in the central hub of your home to maximize its organization potential. You'll be amazed at all the ways a chalkboard wall can help organize your life once it's installed!

WHAT YOU'LL NEED

1 (½-pint) tub spackle

Putty knife

1 piece medium grade sandpaper

1 (18" × 36") tack cloth

1 (1.88" × 180') roll painter's tape

1 (6' × 9') drop cloth

1 (1-quart) can chalkboard paint

1 (1-pint) plastic paint cup

1 (2") angled paintbrush

1 (1-quart) paint tray

1 (1-quart) plastic paint tray liner

1 (9") paint roller frame

1 (9") foam paint roller cover

Chalk

Chalkboard eraser

INSTRUCTIONS

1. Apply the spackle to any nail holes or other holes in the wall using the putty knife and allow to fully dry according to package directions. Using the sandpaper, sand down the spackle and any bumps or imperfections and wipe with a tack cloth to remove all dirt and dust.

2. Tape off the area you wish to paint with painter's tape, and seal the tape edges with the putty knife so the paint doesn't bleed underneath. Lay down your drop cloth to protect the floor.

3. If you have tight spaces or corners, pour some chalkboard paint into a plastic cup and start by covering the areas with paint that will not be easily reached by the paint roller. Once the edges are done, pour the paint into the tray, coat your paint roller with paint, and roll a first coat onto the wall evenly and lightly. You'll want to make big strokes in the shape of a W until the entire area is covered. Let dry the amount of time recommended on the paint can between coats, approximately thirty minutes between coats.

4. Once dry, lightly sand if any imperfections remain and wipe off dust with a tack cloth. Follow with a second coat, let dry, and then follow with a third coat after that. Approximately ten minutes after the last coat, carefully remove the painter's tape while the surface is still slightly wet.

5. Once fully dry (about twenty-four hours later), prep the surface for writing by seasoning it with chalk. Take a piece of chalk and hold it sideways. Rub it all over the wall until it's covered in chalk. Use the eraser to remove the chalk and you're ready to use your new chalkboard wall!

Install a wall-mounted plate or spice rack on the side of the island to increase storage space for cutting boards or other attractive pieces. You can also use wall pockets or magazine files (available in office supply stores) for the same function.

Install a towel bar on the side of your island and hang S-hooks from the bar. Use the hooks to hang cutting boards or utensils that have holes on the end. It's a great way to utilize the valuable storage real estate on the side of your island.

Use large horizontal baskets placed between the upper cabinets and the ceiling to hide items that aren't used often, such as bulk paper products, seasonal items, or special serving pieces. Label them with a pretty tag and it becomes decor.

Attach two towel rods across the inside of cabinet doors and tuck pot and pan lids between the rod and the door for a handy way to organize those hard-to-store lids.

Hot glue a clothespin on the inside of your under-the-sink cabinet door and use it to clip rubber gloves used for cleaning or washing dishes. You'll never have to search for your gloves again, plus they'll dry faster this way.

10 WAYS TO ORGANIZE WITH MASON JARS

Mason jars are a household classic and chances are good that you already have several on hand. If not, they can be readily found at supermarkets, craft stores, and online. While breakable, they are made of thicker glass, which means they are fairly sturdy. This makes them ideal for organizing everything from food to office supplies and so much more.

1. Using a hammer and nail, punch holes in the metal disk lid of a mason jar. Fill the jar with toothpicks, salt, pepper, or anything else that could benefit from a shake-top lid and you have a handy shake-top dispenser.

2. Paint the outside of jars with chalk paint and lightly sand over the raised letters to give a distressed finish for storage jars. This lets you know exactly what's in the jar at a glance and easily change the label when you change the contents.

3. Place several larger mason jars horizontally in a wine bottle rack to create pretty storage for art supplies such as markers and colored pencils.

4. Turn the mason jar into a handy sewing kit by placing an old pincushion on top of the metal disk, covering it with a circle of fabric, and placing the metal ring over it. Place spools of thread and needles inside the jar, and your sewing kit is ready.

5. Use large mason jars for pantry storage. Not only will this make your beans and rice look pretty, you can instantly see what's inside as well as how much you have left.

6. Put wire mesh, such as chicken wire, over the top of a jar and cap it with the metal ring to make a toothbrush holder.

7. Place three mason jars in a caddy, fill with spoons, forks, and knives, and use as a utensil carrier for outdoor dining.

8. Beautify your baking supplies by storing them in mason jars. Put cupcake liners, sprinkles, chocolate chips, baking soda, and other baking staples inside and add labels to make identifying them a breeze.

9. Add a soap dispenser top (available online or in craft stores) to a mason jar and fill with your favorite hand soap. You'll save money buying soap in bulk and you'll have an attractive farmhouse-inspired dispenser to beautify your sink area.

10. Make a wall-mounted mason jar organizer that's useful in just about any room. Use a hammer and nail to punch a hole in the backs of plumbing hose mounts and screw them onto a board, then mount the entire piece to the wall. Attach mason jars to the hose mounts and fill with items you wish to organize.

REFRIGERATORS AND
OTHER APPLIANCES

When loading your dishwasher, group similar silverware together in each basket slot so, when you unload, you can grab each utensil type and place it directly where it belongs.

Inexpensive yet sturdy placemats placed on refrigerator shelves make cleaning your fridge a cinch. Don't forget the shelves on the door as well. When a spill occurs or you're cleaning the fridge, simply remove and rinse it for easy cleanup.

Sort the condiments in your fridge into categories such as dressings, spreads, sauces, and sandwich toppings, and then arrange each category together on whichever shelf they best fit. Use a label maker to label the front of the shelf with the category so everyone knows exactly where to find each condiment.

When freezing food you've already prepared, lay the freezer bag flat so it remains that way. Once all the bags are frozen, they are much easier to stack on top of one another.

METAL CAN TO FAUX BOIS UTENSIL HOLDER

This utensil holder started life as a metal can. This is a great way to hold silverware, kitchen tools, or other necessities in a way that turns them into decor. You can use any type of metal can; coffee or juice cans work great, or use a new empty paint can from a home improvement store (which is what I used in this project). I created a fun faux bois (fake wood) pattern, but you can go crazy with dots or stripes. Regardless of how you decorate it, it's going to look great whether it's holding utensils in your kitchen or office supplies on your desk.

WHAT YOU'LL NEED

Newspaper

1 (1-ounce) bottle white 3-D fabric paint

1 (1-quart) paint can, empty and clean

Pencil

1 (8½" × 11") piece of scrap paper

Scissors

1 (12-ounce) can spray paint

INSTRUCTIONS

1. Lay down newspaper to protect your work surface. Using the bottle of 3-D paint, slowly squeeze the paint out of the bottle to make vertical stripes along the outside of the metal can in various sizes; some lines should go all the way from top to

bottom, others ¾ of the way down the can around a painted "knot" that you've created by making a wide dot with the paint. Some lines might go ¼ of the way down and curve around the "knot." Let the paint dry for twenty-four hours, or until dry and not tacky to the touch.

2. Once the puffy paint is dry, trace the base of the metal can with a pencil onto the scrap paper and then use the scissors to cut a circle of scrap paper sized slightly smaller so it fits snugly into the bottom of the can.

3. Go outside and cover a surface with newspaper to protect from overspray. Place the can on the newspaper and spray paint the outside of the entire can in light, even coats until completely covered. It will take two or three coats with ten minutes of drying time in between.

4. Let it dry for approximately twenty-four hours, or until not sticky to the touch. Remove the paper circle and it's ready to go!

PANTRY AND FOOD STORAGE

Storing pantry staples in their original boxes creates visual clutter, as well as making it hard to see how much is left inside. Invest in clear containers with good seals to keep food fresh. You can use a dry erase marker on most smooth plastic surfaces to write the expiration date directly on the container so you know when to replace the food inside.

Reuse glass spice jars, after a thorough cleaning, as containers to store sprinkles. If you have several colors and varieties, they'll look pretty all lined up.

Cookie cutters look attractive when collected and displayed in a large glass jar. Plus, the clear jar makes it easy to see exactly where that cookie cutter is located when reaching inside.

If you have a pantry staple you use often in a specific amount, pour the entire package into a plastic storage container. Then stick a small adhesive-backed hook on the front of the container and hang a measuring cup from it in the size you typically use.

MAGNETIC SPICE TINS

Spices can quickly overwhelm drawers and cabinets. To overcome this clutter, use space-saving magnetic tins that nestle in otherwise unused spots, such as the inside of cabinets or the side of your fridge. Don't let the name fool you—these handy tins can be used for much more than spices. They snap on to magnetic whiteboards, making them perfect for office supplies. They also attach to a sheet of tin in a craft room to display buttons and glitter beautifully. No matter how you use them, I'm sure you'll agree they're an easy way to solve a common storage problem!

WHAT YOU'LL NEED

12 (3-ounce) clear-fronted metal tins, washed and dried

3 (8.5" × 11") magnet sheets with adhesive side

Thin-tipped permanent marker

Scissors

Label maker with label tape

Magnetic surface

INSTRUCTIONS

1. Place the bottom of the metal tins, one at a time, onto the paper backing of the magnet sheet and trace a circle using a thin-tipped permanent marker. Carefully and evenly cut out the circle with your scissors so that it's slightly smaller than the bottom of the tin.

2. Peel the paper backing off the magnet circle and firmly stick the magnet on the back of the tin. Let the adhesive cure according to the package directions.

3. Fill the tin with spices, label the clear front using your label maker, and stick it onto your magnetic surface.

Herbs and spices should be replaced once they lose their fragrance, often after about one year for spices and six months for herbs. Keeping them in tightly sealed containers away from sunlight helps them last longer, but when it comes time to declutter, be sure to do the "sniff test" and toss any that have lost their potency and flavor.

———

Alphabetize your spices and you'll never have to search more than a few seconds for the right one again.

———

If you purchase baggies of spices or spice mixes, install a towel bar on the back of your pantry door and use curtain rings with clips to hang them.

———

Attach a small clear bin to the wall of your pantry and use it to store sauce and seasoning packets. Otherwise they can easily fall through the shelving or get lost so this puts them right at eye level and makes them easy to see.

UNDER-SHELF STORAGE BASKETS

These handy baskets make use of a typically overlooked space: the under-shelf area. Considered organizing gold, the space under your shelves can be used to stash a myriad of items. In your pantry, it's the perfect place for dressing packets, plastic wrap, aluminum foil, baggies, and more. In closets, it provides an area for accessories or winter gear. Use this quick DIY project for any area that has wire shelving and get extra storage right where you need it.

WHAT YOU'LL NEED

1 plastic front load letter tray with holes on the side large enough to fit nylon cable ties

4 (7") nylon cable ties

Scissors

INSTRUCTIONS

1. Place the tray under the shelf.

2. Thread the cable ties through the holes in the tray, one in each of the four corners, so they line up with the wire they are going to wrap around.

3. Loop the cable ties around the wires of the shelf and connect the two ends, pulling tight to secure the tray.

4. Use the scissors to cut the excess length of plastic from the cable ties.

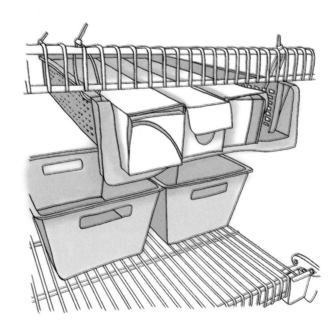

Increase storage space in the pantry by using child-sized pant hangers to hang bags of chips. Suspend them from wire shelving so they'll hang above the shelved products and make use of all available space while keeping the chip bag sealed tight.

Use the back of your pantry door to hang bulky items. Using hooks, hang mixer attachments or colanders, or mesh bags of potatoes, garlic, or onions. Mesh laundry bags work great for this and can be easily laundered as well.

Categorize your canned goods and group accordingly in can dispensers. Label the shelf in front of each dispenser to make it easy to find exactly what you need.

If you don't have a pantry, dedicate space in an easily accessible utility area such as the garage for additional storage of canned food or large-sized paper products such as paper towels.

10 WAYS TO USE UTENSIL DIVIDERS BESIDES HOLDING SILVERWARE

Utensil organizers are often used solely for storing silverware, which doesn't help them live up to their full potential. Truthfully, they can be used in almost every room in the home and we're about to prove it. They can be purchased inexpensively in dollar stores, or you can upgrade to nicer versions for more frequently used areas. You can even make your own (see the Custom Drawer Dividers project in this chapter). They come in a variety of materials and sizes, making them easy to customize to any situation.

1. Junk drawers are no match for the utensil organizer. From hammers to small hardware and anything else your junk drawer may throw your way, a utensil organizer can handle it. Label each section to ensure each item has a neat and tidy home.

2. Use them to store batteries sorted by size. Now you can instantly see you're running low on AAAs well before you need them. Tuck a small screwdriver and battery checker into the organizer as well so all your battery changing supplies are on hand when needed.

3. Toothbrushes and toothpaste are best stored off of bathroom countertops, but you don't want them rolling around in drawers. If sharing a bathroom, assign each person a section of the utensil divider so everyone has a spot to store their items in a way that won't cause cross-contamination.

4. Makeup fits nicely when sorted into the various sections. Storing products this way makes it easy to find the perfect shade of lipstick without having to dig through eyeshadows,

blushes, and more. Plus it offers a space to put your makeup brushes so they don't get other items dirty.

5. Make a candle storage station by storing tapers, tea lights, and lighters in the various parts of the organizer. Make sure the drawer is childproofed if kids are around.

6. The spaces in the dividers are well suited for rolls of thread and sewing needles to create a handy sewing station in a hobby or craft area.

7. If you are a nail polish fanatic, you can lay out your polishes and nail tools in the dividers to make them easy to reach while protecting the drawer from accidental spills.

8. Tuck a utensil organizer in a dresser drawer and fill it with various shades of shoe polish and polishing rags to keep those messy supplies organized neatly and ready to use whenever needed.

9. Nightstands are another spot that tends to gather small bits of clutter. Place a utensil organizer in a nightstand drawer to give your glasses, lip balms, bookmarks, and other stray items a spot to rest.

10. For some reason, office drawer organizers are often *more* expensive than utensil dividers even though they're essentially the same thing. Use the utensil version in your office drawers to beat the pricing game.

DINING ROOM

· · · · · · · · · · · · · · · · · · · ·

When storing tablecloths, folding them in half and then rolling them onto empty wrapping paper rolls prevents most creases.

———

Store cloth napkins and linens nestled in a serving dish to make your serving pieces work double duty when not in use.

———

The dining room is often a place used to store items that aren't frequently used, such as wedding china and family heirlooms. Make over an old hutch using furniture paint then store items such as these inside.

———

Attach cup hooks to the bottom of a shelf in your hutch to hang punch cups, teacups, or mugs with plenty of room to spare below.

———

If you don't have a hutch, a dresser works nicely to store items such as silverware, napkins, napkin rings, taper candles, and more. Smaller items can be placed in the shallower drawers up top, and tablecloths and large servingware can go in deeper drawers. The top surface can be used as a serving space when entertaining.

03

BATHROOMS

Bathrooms may not be the most exciting spaces in our home, but it's hard to imagine life without one. With so many items squeezed into a typically small space, the space is easily overwhelmed with personal care products, toiletries, and towels. And if the bathroom is shared with several household members, you have a bona fide organization challenge on your hands. However, these hacks will help you get everything so organized that even the most industrious bathroom cabinet snooper will be impressed with your amazing storage skills.

COUNTERTOPS, SINKS, AND VANITIES

Basic supplies such as cotton swabs and cotton balls look fancy when decanted into glass jars. This trick makes your countertops look organized, and the glass jars look beautiful lined up or grouped together.

Bobby pins always seem to be missing when you need one and everywhere when you don't. Put your medicine cabinet door to work by attaching a strip of magnetic tape to the inside of the door and using it to secure those little buggers.

Collect hair ties by clipping them onto a carabiner and you won't have to deal with scattered hair elastics again.

If you have kids, assign each one a color-coded cup to rinse after brushing so there will be no more mix-ups.

Label the toothpaste so everyone has their own tube to avoid cross-contamination. This is especially helpful when someone gets sick and you're trying to protect the entire household.

TWO-TIERED STORAGE TRAYS

Beautifully organize your bathroom countertops with this quick DIY project that provides plenty of extra space for frequently used products. In minutes, you'll have a two-tiered stand that will make even the most common items look special and puts them right at your fingertips.

WHAT YOU'LL NEED

1 (2-ounce) tube clear craft glue, industrial strength
Candlestick with flat top
One large plate
One medium-sized plate

INSTRUCTIONS

1. Carefully place a line of glue around the bottom of the base of the candlestick.

2. Place the bottom of the candlestick on the top of the large plate directly in the middle, applying pressure for approximately five seconds so it sticks.

3. Place a line of glue around the top of the candlestick.

4. Place the middle of the bottom of the medium-sized plate onto the top of the candlestick and apply pressure for approximately five seconds.

5. Let dry approximately one hour, or according to package directions. Once fully dry, place on your bathroom countertop and arrange frequently used items on the plates.

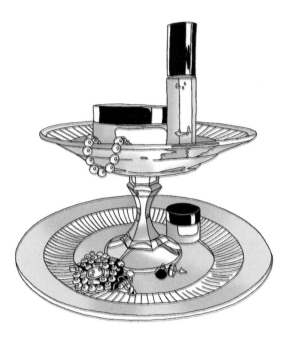

If you have a large nail polish collection, display it elegantly by carefully placing the bottles in a large glass cookie or candy jar.

———

Use ice cube trays to organize small eyeshadows by tucking them into the cups in each tray. This method makes it easy to immediately see and choose the right eyeshadow color.

———

Shallow shelves such as those made for spices provide extra storage for sponges and other small items when mounted on the inside of the cabinet door under the sink.

———

If you have small soaps, place them in open glass jars to both look pretty and scent the room.

———

Adhesive-backed clips can hold toothbrushes and razors to the back of your medicine cabinet door. This keeps them off the counters and makes everything neat and tidy.

———

If you do any magazine reading in the bathroom, hang a wooden clothes hanger from the knob of the cabinet door under the sink. Slide magazines over the bottom of the hanger for an attractive magazine holder.

MAGNETIC
MAKEUP BOARD

When short on space, every hack counts. This quick solution frees up counter or drawer space, puts makeup within reach, and provides an easy way to display all your makeup options in one place. Once finished, your entire palette is right there to choose from when applying your makeup each day.

WHAT YOU'LL NEED

1 package (4 pairs) medium-sized adhesive picture hanging strips
1 (18" × 13") metal cookie sheet
Level
Pencil
1 package (24) adhesive-backed magnet dots

INSTRUCTIONS

1. Open the package of picture hanging strips. Press two strips together face-to-face until they attach to each other. You will now have four sets of two strips each with the paper backing facing out.

2. Flip the cookie sheet facedown so the back of the sheet is facing up. Peel one backing from each set of hanging strips and attach one to each of the four corners of the cookie sheet on the side facing you.

3. Place the back of the cookie sheet on the wall where you will want to hang it. Place the level on top and adjust until it's perfectly straight. Lightly trace the top line of the cookie sheet with a pencil and take the cookie sheet off the wall. Remove the other side of the adhesive backing from the picture hanging strips and place the cookie sheet on the wall with the hanging strips against the wall, lining it up with the mark you just made. Apply pressure to each corner for approximately thirty seconds to ensure the adhesive sticks.

4. Peel off the paper covering the adhesive on each dot magnet and firmly attach to the back of each container of makeup. Press for approximately ten seconds or according to package directions. Once cured (approximately one hour), arrange on the cookie sheet by the type of makeup and then by color.

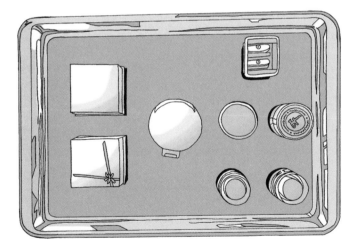

Pedestal sinks sure are beautiful...until you need to store something, that is. Adding a fabric "skirt" using hook and loop strips around the sink edge adds an extra bit of storage underneath.

Attach adhesive-backed hooks inside the cabinet door under the sink to hold your bulky styling tools by their loops.

Hang wire baskets using adhesive-backed hooks on the side of your cabinet to hold styling tools such as brushes, hair dryers, and curling irons.

If you tend to lose track of time in the morning, hang a clock in the bathroom so you can stick to your schedule. You'll never get caught up singing into your hairbrush again, or maybe you will, but at least you'll allot the proper amount of time for it.

Mount lightweight plastic cups to the inside of the vanity cabinet door with Velcro strips to organize toothbrushes and keep your counters mess-free.

A thin picture rail shelf is the perfect size for votive holders or thin bottles such as perfumes, sprays, and colognes. These shelves fit in tight spaces, making them a useful and attractive addition to the vanity area in your bathroom.

TURN BASKETS INTO SHELVES

This easy trick for providing extra storage is perfect for small spaces such as bathrooms and pantries. The best part is you can choose the baskets that fit your style and match your decor. If you plan to store lighter items like rolled towels and toilet paper rolls, you can go with basic woven baskets. Heavier items do best with sturdy wire baskets or even wooden crates. Consider using the basket for only one function, such as exclusively for rolled hand towels. This helps prevent them from getting overloaded.

WHAT YOU'LL NEED

1 (10" × 12") rectangular woven basket

1 (10" × 18") rectangular woven basket

Level

Pencil

Stud finder

4 (1") screws

Cordless drill with driver bit

INSTRUCTIONS

1. Place the bottom of your basket against the wall in the exact location you wish to hang it. Use a level to make sure it's straight and lightly draw an outline around it in pencil.

2. Use the stud finder to locate the studs near where you marked. Mark the studs with your pencil.

3. Put the bottom of your basket against the wall within the outline. Using the screws and cordless drill with driver bit attached, screw the bottom of the basket into the studs as close to the four corners of the basket as possible. Make sure not to drive the screws all the way in, just far enough to hold the basket tightly to the wall.

TOILETRIES AND PERSONAL CARE PRODUCTS

Use picnic baskets or other lidded baskets to house toilet paper and other bathroom necessities so that they are readily available yet out of sight.

Store products in medium-sized lidded plastic bins in the linen closet or under the sink and label with categories such as *first aid*, *medications*, and *personal care products*.

If you take a daily medication, use a marker to draw a chart with dates on the side of the bottle and mark off each day you take it. This is especially helpful for short-term medications or when there's multiple caretakers dispensing it.

Use daylight saving time as a reminder to check the expiration date on medications. Whether the clock is "falling back" or "springing forward," it's a great way to remember to check the dates and discard anything that's past its prime.

10 WAYS TO ORGANIZE USING TRAYS

There's just something about a tray that makes even a group of ordinary objects look organized. Trays also provide a clearly defined home for items, which we know is one of the Ten Commandments of Organizing. Plus, they can be found in many sizes and colors to fit any decor. The possibilities may be endless, but here are ten ways to start:

1. If you entertain outdoors often, keep shatterproof plates and cups on a large tray along with a caddy with silverware and some citronella candles. When you're ready to set the outdoor table, everything is ready to go.

2. If beauty products are taking over your bathroom countertops, a tray will rein them back in.

3. Place any essential cooking items on a tray next to the stove so your oils, vinegar, salt, and pepper can be accessed quickly and easily.

4. For parents with a kiddo who loves to play with LEGOs, a large tray can serve as a flat surface for building. It can be easily moved out of the way when it's not being used.

5. Make a coffee or tea station by grouping all your supplies on a tray atop your kitchen countertop.

6. Use trays to delineate the various areas of a drink cart, such as cocktail supplies, glasses, and bottles.

7. Turn an upholstered ottoman into a coffee table with the addition of a large, sturdy tray on top to hold drinks and remotes.

8. Paint a tray with chalkboard paint and mount it to the wall to create a memo board.

9. Use a tray to display and showcase a collection and it will instantly look pulled together, purposeful, and have the most impact.

10. Boot trays are specifically made to keep muddy shoes from dirtying floors and make the area look tidy. Keep one by every entrance to your home to stop dirt in its tracks.

Decorate a tall, wide canister (such as the type oatmeal comes in) with wrapping or contact paper and use it to store rolls of toilet paper.

It's important to have a first aid kit. Place first aid essentials such as Band-Aids, rubbing alcohol, and gauze in a toolbox so you can grab it quickly in an emergency.

If you have a plethora of product samples, don't put them away in a bin. Instead, store them where you'll use them. For example, place shampoo samples in the shower.

If you take frequent baths, keep a large glass jar of bath salts on the countertop with a scoop inside and scent it with essential oils. Instant spa!

SHOWERS, BATHTUBS, AND TOWELS

Install a second shower curtain rod on the inside wall of your bathtub specifically for hanging clothing to dry. Now all of the water will drip right into the tub.

Use a few plastic buckets with holes to store bath toys when not in use.

Stick adhesive-backed hooks on the shower wall away from the showerhead and hang bath poufs that are color-coded for each family member to avoid a pileup.

Keep the shower neat by giving each person in your household a small shower caddy and storing them under the sink when not in use. The tub and shower stay clear and it makes cleaning a cinch.

Choose a different color for each member of the family and sew a seam binding or washable ribbon in that color to the corner of each towel to make it easy to hang.

PERSONALIZED TOWEL HOOKS

It's hard to keep track of what towel belongs to which family member in a shared bathroom space. These personalized towel hangers solve that problem by using craft store wooden letters and adhesive-backed hooks for a clever custom towel spot. If your household has members with the same first initial, you can use the initial of a nickname instead or decorate the hooks with different paint colors or stickers (dinosaurs, anyone?). Best of all, there will be no more mixing up towels once everyone gets in the habit of knowing exactly where to find their own.

WHAT YOU'LL NEED

Newspaper

1 (2-ounce) bottle craft paint

1 (1") paintbrush

Medium-sized wood letter, precut with notch for hanging

1 large adhesive-backed hook

1 pair of adhesive-backed picture hanging strips

Stud finder

1 (1") screw

Cordless drill with driver bit

INSTRUCTIONS

1. Lay down newspaper to protect your workspace. Using your bottle of paint and paintbrush, paint the letter with two or

three coats of paint until the wood grain no longer shows through, with about twenty minutes drying time in between coats. Let dry twenty-four hours after the final coat.

2. Remove one side of the backing from the adhesive strip and apply it to the back of the hook. Then remove the other side of the backing and firmly press the hook onto the letter for approximately thirty seconds.

3. Attach one set of adhesive picture hanging strips to the back of the letter toward the bottom and remove the backing.

4. Use your stud finder to locate a stud on which to hang the letter. Drill a screw into the stud using the driver bit on your cordless drill so that approximately ¼" is left exposed. Place the notch in the letter onto the screw.

5. Press the area with the adhesive-backed picture strip to the wall firmly for thirty seconds to provide extra stability. Let the adhesive-backed hook cure for at least twenty-four hours before you hang anything from your personalized letter hook.

10 WAYS TO REPURPOSE LADDERS

Ladders can be found in almost any garage or storage shed, so let's make them work double duty. With a few tweaks, they are especially great for display and storage. You can use a vintage ladder for a relaxed vibe or make your own with the Blanket and Towel Display Ladder tutorial in Chapter 4. No matter which type you choose, you're going to love this on-trend household workhorse.

1. Create a tall and chic bookcase using two stepladders of equal height and some planks. Place the ladders parallel to one another with the steps facing each other. Attach planks across the steps for the shelves, and voila, a nice tall bookcase!

2. A smaller version of this is to use just one open stepladder and place it with one flat side against the wall. Slide planks over the rungs on both sides to create shelves down the middle.

3. Take a cue from fancy stationery stores and use ladders to hold wrapping paper draped over the rungs.

4. Towel storage is easy when you drape towels over ladder rungs in the bathroom. You can mount it to the wall or use a leaning one.

5. If the rungs on your ladder are thin, you can use S-hooks to hang just about anything from them—mugs, scarves, belts, you name it.

6. Hang a ladder parallel with the ceiling and create a pot rack by using S-hooks to hang pots and pans.

7. Similarly, you can hang it from the ceiling and use it as a drying rack for laundry.

8. Lean a ladder against the wall and slide magazines over each rung for a cool and unique magazine rack.

9. If a temporary wardrobe rack is needed (such as a rack to hang clothes at a yard sale), set up two stepladders of equal height and use duct tape to secure a broom handle in between the topmost steps. Hang your clothes on the pole and you have a handy hack to store or display clothing.

10. If you have high-heel shoes, you can slide the heel over the rungs of an extension-style ladder with the toes pointing down for vertical shoe storage.

DRIP-DRY BATHTUB TOY HOLDER

Bath toys. Those slippery little guys are kind of a nightmare to deal with, especially when someone wants to take a shower or clean the tub. This project makes the tub easier to clean and puts the toys right within arm's reach for kids. Plus, toys can drip-dry right into the tub instead of all over the bathroom floor.

WHAT YOU'LL NEED

1 (72") adjustable tension shower rod

1 package (12) shower curtain rings

3 plastic baskets with holes on their side large enough to fit shower rings

INSTRUCTIONS

1. Place one end of the tension rod against the wall, above the side of the tub but low enough for kids to reach into the baskets that will hang from it. Extend it the length of the tub from wall to wall, and then firmly push it down into place and make sure it's tight and secure.

2. Open the package of shower curtain rings. On one side of the basket, insert one ring into each of the top corner holes, a total of two rings. Repeat with the other two baskets.

3. Clip the shower curtain rings onto the tension rod with the basket facing into the tub, and then close the rings.

4. Fill the baskets with all of the loose toys that once scattered the bottom of your bathtub.

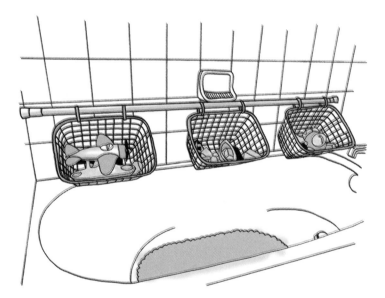

Add an extra towel bar to the back of bathroom doors to increase the amount of space in your bathroom.

———

Use a wall-mounted wine rack and fill with rolled towels. It looks like a spa and provides extra storage.

———

When placing towels in the closet, do so with the folded edge facing out. Not only does it look neater, but it ensures you'll only grab one.

———

Sometimes the right hook placement makes all the difference. Having a towel hook right outside the shower ensures towels are within reach and you won't drip water across the floor.

———

Jazz up your bathroom decor with nontraditional hooks for your towels. Use metal rake heads or vintage doorknobs to make towel hooks. You can even stretch some rope between two large eye hooks to create a handy place to drape towels.

———

Keep a bath caddy handy under the sink, filled with bath salts, a book, and perhaps a candle. Consider it your own personal spa in a box.

04

LIVING ROOM, ENTRYWAY, AND MEDIA

Living rooms and entryways can be clutter magnets. It is essential, therefore, to keep these spaces organized in order to manage your time and busy life. The hacks in this chapter are designed to keep clutter under control and help you implement a system where everyone can easily find keys, shoes, and remotes without having to spend precious time searching the whole house. Instead, you'll have time to use these areas as intended: for living in and enjoying your home!

LIVING ROOMS

Cords are a necessary evil in your living room, but that doesn't mean you need to see these eyesores every day. Hide cords by attaching small adhesive-backed hooks to the back of your TV stand or end tables. Wires can now run behind the furniture, making the view cord-free, and much more peaceful.

A storage ottoman can be a brilliant way to organize game systems and remotes. Attach a piece of Velcro to the back of each remote and its matching piece to one of the four sides on the inside of the ottoman... You can also store video game controllers and DVDs in the ottoman for an invisible media and gaming center.

Baskets are the epitome of hide-in-plain-sight storage. You can match them to your decorating style: wicker for farmhouse, woven for eclectic, clean lines for modern, and more. If you don't like the color, spray paint or dip dye them!

Use baskets to stash items for a clean, uncluttered appearance on the outside (and storage ninja on the inside). Tuck them into bookcases, under benches or console tables, on side tables, or on top of armoires.

Paint the wall behind your TV black or charcoal to help it blend in and provide an uncluttered visual space.

———

Collections of smaller-sized items such as shells, corks, ticket stubs, or beach glass can be stored in tall glass jars or vases. Group them together on a shelf for a purposeful and elegant display.

———

Don't let your remotes hang out on your coffee table, all lonely and scared. Collect them in large bowls, trays, or footed urns for storage with style.

———

Use Velcro to attach video game controllers to the back of media cabinet doors for a quick way to store them when not in use.

———

Attach a power strip to the underside of end tables for an out-of-sight spot to plug in lamps and electronics.

———

Coffee tables can serve as storage too. Consider using an old trunk with a lid that opens. The top tray inside can hold books and remotes while the rest can serve as ample storage for blankets and throw pillows.

10 USES FOR TV ARMOIRES

There was a time when armoires could be found in many homes because they served a purpose of hiding televisions while providing storage space. With the advent of wall-mounted TVs, they have become less popular though not less useful. The large area behind the doors is wonderfully versatile, and the drawers below provide abundant additional storage. Before you ditch your armoire, here's ten more ways to use them besides housing TVs. You may even find yourself scouting thrift stores for more of them!

1. If you have the space, place one in your kitchen for storing small appliances, cookbooks, and pots and pans. You can convert the open space on top into a memo area with the addition of a corkboard or by painting it with chalkboard paint.

2. If you no longer need one to hold a television, put a clothing bar across the top of the interior to create an extra wardrobe space for hanging clothes. The drawers can also be used for additional clothing storage.

3. Even if the TV no longer lives inside, armoires are perfect for storing DVDs, video game systems, and board games.

4. Whether you have a fully dedicated craft room or just a corner to serve that purpose, armoires are an awesome way to store all your supplies. Your sewing machine can go in the cabinet space, with fabric and craft supplies in the drawers below. Mount spool holders or even a pegboard to the upper inside area to further organize everything.

5. Convert an armoire into a desk by placing your computer in the top space and a keyboard in the drawer underneath. Tuck office supplies and paper into the drawers below.

6. If you're lucky enough to have a large bathroom, make it look grand with the addition of an armoire. There's plenty of space for linens and towels as well as personal care products and styling tools.

7. Those who live in climates with cold winters can relate to the game of winter blanket bingo. Armoires can be used to store out-of-season linens when you need both winter and summer bedding.

8. Armoires can convert into handy potting stations. The open space is roomy enough for potting plants, and the drawers are perfect for stashing supplies and work gloves. Hang tools on the inside of the doors for easy access while working.

9. Armoires are great as a spare pantry. The open area can serve as a space for holding canisters and larger boxes like cereal while the drawers create a way to store cans and other pantry staples.

10. If you love to entertain, you'll appreciate the extra space an armoire provides. Convert the top section to a beverage or serving area, and hide tablecloths, linens, and safely stored china below.

When shopping for coffee tables, look for ones with space to hide baskets underneath. The top will get used as normal, but the bottom can become the perfect spot for board games, remotes, and books.

———

Corral your remotes in a silverware caddy with a handle so it's easy to store and carry away when you're entertaining or need space on your coffee table.

———

If you have too many remotes to count, invest in a universal remote. It takes a few minutes to set up, but once ready you'll have one remote to rule them all.

———

If your couch sits against a wall, try pulling it out a few inches and adding a console table behind it. It's mostly hidden so the style doesn't matter, but it becomes a handy resting spot for lamps, remotes, and drinks.

———

If you have young kids, designate a makeshift play area in the living room. Cover it in kid-friendly material such as a rug or foam squares and have a large basket in which to throw all the toys at the end of a play session.

WOODEN CRATE BOOKSHELF

Don't let the simplicity of this project fool you: These easy-to-build bookcases pack a huge organization punch. If you need more space, go double wide with two stacks of three crates. Or go low with four stacks of two crates for shelving that fits under windows. Paint or stain them to match your decor or keep them in a natural wood tone for an industrial chic look. If you're using this bookshelf in an area with pets or children, you may want to strap the bookshelf to the wall for added stability.

WHAT YOU'LL NEED

3 (18" × 12" × 9½") wooden crates

1 sheet medium grade sandpaper

1 (18" × 36") tack cloth

Newspaper

1 (4-ounce) bottle wood glue

4 spring clamps

Ruler

Pencil

Cordless drill with driver bit

1 pack of 4 (2" × ½") mending braces with screws

INSTRUCTIONS

1. Sand the crates with the sandpaper. The crates come with a rough finish so you'll want to get a smooth surface to prevent splinters. Clean off sawdust with a tack cloth.

2. Protect your floor with newspaper. Place one crate on top of the newspaper with the opening on the side and the long (18") side against the floor. Squeeze a line of wood glue along the middle of each of the top slats.

3. Place the second crate on top facing the same direction, checking the back side of the crates to make sure they are perfectly lined up and flush with each other. Clamp the crates together with two spring clamps.

4. Repeat the same process, gluing and clamping the third crate on top of the second. Let the glue dry for twenty-four hours.

5. Once dry, remove the clamps and carefully place the unit with the open side down on the floor. Use your ruler to measure ½" in from the bottom left edge of the top crate and make a mark there with your pencil then do the same from the top left edge of the middle crate.

6. Line up your mending brace with those two marks. You may need to adjust the placement to ensure you won't be screwing into the spot where the manufacturer has stapled in the wooden slats.

7. Use the cordless drill to drive the screws through each hole in the brace so it attaches the left sides of the top and middle crates together.

8. Repeat this process to attach another mending brace on the back of the top two crates on the right side, adding the brace above the bottom right edge of the top crate and below the top right edge of the second crate. Repeat again to attach the middle crate to the bottom crate.

ENTRYWAYS

Make your own boot tray by placing river rocks on a rimmed cookie sheet. This makes the perfect spot to store wet or dirty boots because air can circulate underneath to encourage drying.

Add a basket filled with slippers by the front door to encourage your family to take off their shoes while inside and help them relax after a long day.

Place an umbrella stand by the front door to keep floors dry as well as a reminder to grab one on the way out on rainy days.

Invest in wood hangers for your coat closet. It makes your closet look neater and protects your clothing better as well.

If you have a large entryway but no coat closet, get an attractive stand-alone wardrobe or retrofit an armoire with a hanging bar.

ENTRYWAY KEY HOLDER FROM REPURPOSED DRAWER

We all know that person who never seems to be able to find his or her keys when needed (for some of us that person may be ourselves). Hang this key holder next to the front door and there will be no more misplaced keys or excuses for being late.

WHAT YOU'LL NEED

Cordless drill with driver bit

Medium drawer (I used a drawer that measured 15" × 13" × 4")

1 (⅜") drill bit

Newspaper

1 (2") paintbrush

1 (1-quart) can latex paint

Ruler

Pencil

6 (1½") cup hooks

Level

4 (1¼") hollow wall anchors with screws

INSTRUCTIONS

1. Using the cordless drill with driver bit attached, remove any hardware such as sliders and drawer pulls from the drawer.

2. Lay down newspaper to protect your workspace. Using the paintbrush, paint the drawer with two or three coats of paint until completely covered and let dry twenty-four hours or until completely dry to the touch.

3. Place the drawer so that the bottom is flat on a table with the open side facing up. Measure the width of the interior of the bottom of the drawer then divide that number by four. We'll call that distance W". This is going to be the spacing between each cup hook. Next, measure the length of the drawer and divide that by three. We'll call this L". This will be the spacing between the two rows. Now use your ruler to measure down L" and draw a faint line horizontally across the drawer with your pencil. Measure W" along that line and mark a spot on the line then repeat until you have three spots equidistant from each other on the line.

4. Repeat the whole process, measuring L" down from the first line.

5. Manually screw the cup hooks where you have made the marks by applying pressure and turning the screw end of the cup hook into the mark until it's firmly screwed into the drawer. Check the back of the drawer as you screw in the cup hooks to make sure the screw end doesn't protrude from the back.

6. Place the drawer on the wall near the entryway and use the level to make sure it's straight. Use the cordless drill with the drill bit attached to make ⅜" pilot holes through the four corners of the drawer and into the wall.

7. With your pencil, mark where the top two corners of the drawer meet the wall and remove the drawer from the wall. Then follow the package instructions for inserting the wall anchors into the wall where the pilot holes were drilled.

8. Using the pencil marks for placement, hold up the drawer again on the wall. Put a screw in each pilot hole and screw them one at a time into the wall anchors using the cordless drill.

Old fashioned stand-alone coat racks were once popular for a reason: They're a functional way to hang hats, leashes, scarves, and accessories...and yes, even coats! Purchase one retail or scour vintage shops until you find one that fits your style.

Mount a napkin holder to the wall next to your front door to use as a mail sorter and organizer.

Attach a wire wall pocket by your front door for outgoing mail and notes. This pocket also makes for a handy place to hang keys using S-hooks.

DO-IT-YOURSELF DROP ZONE

The drop zone has quickly become an essential part of an organized home. Whether you're lucky enough to have a large mudroom or you have to carve out an area in an unorthodox place near the entryway, creating a catch-it-all zone for stuff when leaving and entering will help busy families stay sane. Use it as a place to hang keys, coats, and backpacks as well as a spot to stash winter mittens or summer sunglasses, shoes, and umbrellas. Basically, if it's something you grab on the way out the door or an item that needs to get dropped on the way in, it belongs here.

WHAT YOU'LL NEED

12' measuring tape

Pencil

1 (9½" × 46" × 1") shelf with precut notches for mounting

Level

3 (1¼") wall anchors with screws

Hot glue gun

2 hot glue sticks

6 (4" × 6") chalkboard signs

3 (9" × 15" × 8") baskets

1 box chalk

3 (4") wall mount coat hooks with screws

Cordless drill with driver bit

3 adhesive-backed hanging strips

Newspaper

3 (12" × 18" × 9") wooden crates

1 (4-ounce) bottle wood glue

1 (3") notched plastic trowel

4 spring clamps

1 pack of 4 (2" × ½") mending braces with screws

INSTRUCTIONS

1. Using your measuring tape, measure 62" up from the floor and use the pencil to mark where you want to hang the shelf.

2. Place the shelf at that mark, using your level to make sure it's straight, and draw a line on the wall using the top of the shelf as a guide. Remove the shelf from wall, then measure the distance between the mounting holes on the back of the shelf and the side of the shelf with your ruler. Using the measurements you just found, mark the spots on the line on the wall where the mounting holes will align. Following the package directions for the wall anchors, attach the anchors to the wall in those locations, leaving about ¼" of the screws protruding. Hang the shelf on the screws.

3. Insert a hot glue stick into the hot glue gun and plug it in so it heats up, approximately five minutes. Using the glue gun, apply glue to the back of three of the chalkboard signs and attach them to the front of each basket by pressing down until dry, about thirty seconds. Place the baskets on the shelf and label the chalkboard signs in chalk with either a person's name or a description of what will be stored inside.

4. Using the measuring tape and pencil, measure 6" below the shelf and mark where you want to hang the hooks. Leave enough space between the shelf and the hook for the remaining chalkboard signs and evenly space them along the wall so they are below that person's basket on the shelf. Attach the hooks to the wall by drilling pilot holes and then using screws to mount each hook.

5. Write the name of each person in chalk on the remaining chalkboards. Using the adhesive-backed hanging strips, hang the chalkboard above that person's hook and below the shelf.

6. Protect your floor with newspaper. Place one crate on top of the newspaper with the short (12") side against the floor and the opening facing you. Squeeze wood glue across the face of the side facing up and spread an even layer with the notched plastic trowel.

7. Place the second crate on top so the two 12" sides are on top of one another and facing the same direction. Check the back side of the crates to make sure they are perfectly lined up and flush with each other. Clamp the crates together with two spring clamps. Repeat the same process, gluing and clamping the third crate on top of the second. Let the glue dry for twenty-four hours.

8. Once dry, remove the clamps and carefully place the unit horizontally in front of you with the open sides facing the floor. Use your ruler to measure ½" in from the top right edge of the first crate and make a mark there with your pencil, then do the same from the top left edge of the middle crate. Line up your mending brace with those two marks. You may need to adjust placement to ensure you won't be screwing into the spot where the manufacturer has stapled in the wooden slats.

9. Use the cordless drill to drive screws through each hole in the brace so it attaches the first and middle crates together in that top corner.

10. Repeat this process to attach another mending brace on the bottom edges of the first and middle crates, adding the brace to the bottom right side of the first crate and the bottom left side of the middle crate. Repeat again to attach the middle crate to the third crate in the top and bottom edges.

11. Flip crates so the opening is facing forward and they are horizontally lined up under the hooks, and load up with shoes. Now each person has his or her own "zone" for storing belongings.

Life can be busy, so it's a good idea to have bags prepacked for common activities. That way you can easily grab and go. When you return home, make sure to restock the bag and put it back in the correct spot.

Don't let open space under the stairs go to waste. Tuck a bookcase or a clothing rod inside or outfit it with hooks and baskets for a faux mudroom.

Labeling keys takes out the guesswork when you need to find the right one. Use nail polish on the top of your keys create a color-code system. You'll be able to easily identify each one at a glance.

An easy and attractive way to store shoes is to hang Shaker-style pegs near floor level and hang shoes from each peg.

10 WAYS TO HACK A WOODEN CRATE

Plain wooden crates can be found at just about any craft store. They're great for organizing because they can be decorated to match your personal style with just a good sanding and a coat of paint, stain, or stenciled wording on the side. Don't let their plain exterior fool you: wooden crates are the chameleons of the organizing world and can store just about anything!

1. Add casters to the bottom for rolling storage crates that tuck easily under console tables, beneath desks, and in closets.

2. Add table legs (found in the hardware store) to the long side of a rectangular crate (with the open side facing out) and it becomes a new end table with plenty of storage to stash remotes and other common items.

3. Place a rectangular crate horizontally on a table with the open side facing you. Add beverage dispensers on top and fill the inside with glasses to create an easy beverage station for your next event.

4. Decorate and label plain crates to create hidden storage on bookcases, shelves, or kitchen carts. They're perfect for storing small appliances you don't use every day like juicers or mixers.

5. Place the tall side up for an impromptu nightstand or end table.

6. Add diagonally crossed shelves or a thrifted wine rack inside a crate to store wine bottles horizontally.

7. Easily sort your recycling by placing two or three crates side by side on the floor of the garage. Toss any recyclables in, and then carry them to the bins on recycling day. Add casters to the bottom of a crate to make it easy to roll it wherever it's needed.

8. Create screwdriver storage by placing a rectangular wooden crate on your workbench with the opening facing you. Drill holes down through the top of a wooden crate large enough to allow shanks of screwdrivers to fit through without falling out. You now have an easy way to store tools and a bonus storage space for gloves, sanding disks, or hardware.

9. Flip a crate upside down and add a pillow or cushion on top to make instant seating for kids that doubles as storage when not in use.

10. Stack two large crates on top of one another and attach them with mending braces in their back corners. Then stack and attach two more separately. Connect the two stacks with a board or flat door on top to create an instant desk with storage on either side.

MEDIA

· · · · · · · · · · ·

Organize magazines by season, not by title. You can pull them out and find seasonally appropriate information instead of having to dig through your magazines one by one.

———

Pull out your favorite ideas and recipes from magazines and organize them in a binder using plastic sleeves and index dividers. For a few hours of sweat equity, you'll have your own "book" personalized with your favorite articles and ideas.

———

While this hack is controversial in some book-worshiping circles, one way to make your book collection double as decor is to organize them by spine color. It really pulls the collection together and allows them to stand out. You'll soon grow accustomed to recognizing the books by color and it might even spur you to reread a few as well!

———

If you have any old CDs or DVDs hanging around, consider tossing out the cases and collecting the discs in one large binder outfitted with sleeves specifically made for that purpose. This takes up much less storage space as we transition ourselves into all-digital media.

UPCYCLED REMOTE CONTROL STORAGE BOX

No matter how beautifully you decorate your living room, chances are there's one big eyesore: remote controls. An attractive jewelry box, easily found at your local thrift or craft store, is a great way to hide these unsightly technological necessities. Even better, you can use your own personal style to make it part of the decor.

WHAT YOU'LL NEED

1 jewelry box (approximately 9" × 5½")

1 piece medium grade sandpaper

1 (18" × 36") tack cloth

Newspaper

1 (2-ounce) bottle craft paint

1 (2") paintbrush

Ruler

Scissors

1 or 2 pieces (12" × 12") scrapbook paper

1 (4-ounce) container Mod Podge

Hot glue gun

2 hot glue sticks

Decorative object such as a rock or shell that's smaller than the box (I used a geode slice)

INSTRUCTIONS

1. Remove all of the interior trays and linings from the jewelry box. Sand it down and wipe off the dust with a tack cloth. Lay newspaper down to protect your workspace. Paint the box with your paintbrush, using two or three light, even coats (with twenty minutes drying time in between) until completely covered. Let dry completely, about twenty-four hours.

2. Using the ruler, measure the interior of both the lid and the base of the jewelry box.

3. Use the scissors to cut two pieces of scrapbook paper, one the size of the lid interior and one the size of the base interior. Using your paintbrush, spread a light layer of Mod Podge to the backs of the two pieces, and place them inside the box in their respective locations. Push out all of the air bubbles for a clean look.

4. Insert a hot glue stick into the hot glue gun and plug it in so it heats up, approximately five minutes. Using the glue gun, add a dab of glue to the bottom of your decorative object and firmly attach the decorative object to the top of the box by applying pressure until the glue cools, about thirty seconds. Let it dry for approximately twenty-four hours.

5. Gather up your remotes and place them inside their new home.

Make it a project to go digital by transferring videos onto hard drives or cloud storage. At some point soon everything will be digital, so it's a good idea to transfer them while the equipment is still available.

———

Stack vintage or large coffee table books flat upon each other instead of vertically. This flat stack is better for their spines and creates a high-end designer look in your living room.

———

Dedicate a basket in your home for library books. All library books should be collected in this area whenever they aren't actively being read. This avoids them getting mixed up with your other books and makes them easy to grab and return.

———

For those with a large book collection, organize your books by genre. Put a color-coded label on the spines and group each category together.

BLANKET AND TOWEL DISPLAY LADDER

Wooden display ladders are functional yet beautiful ways to hang blankets and towels, and they fit into small spaces where extra storage is often needed. You can make one for just a few dollars and use it in just about any room in your home. This is a great way to display hanging items elegantly and attractively.

WHAT YOU'LL NEED

2 (5' × 2" × 2") wood furring strips

5 (18" × 2" × 2") wood furring strips

Ruler

Pencil

Cordless drill with driver bit

10 (2") screws

INSTRUCTIONS

1. Lay the wood pieces flat on your workspace. Place the two 5' long pieces of furring strips parallel to each other—these will be the legs of the ladder.

2. On both legs, use the ruler to measure 6" down from the top and mark a dot on the outside with your pencil. Then, again on both legs, measure 6" up from the bottom and mark a dot on the outside with your pencil. This will be where your top and bottom rungs will go.

3. Using your ruler and pencil, measure and mark every 12" from the top rung to the bottom rung. This will be where the remaining three rungs will be placed. When finished, you should have equally spaced marks on each leg.

4. Now, place the first 18" length of furring strip between the highest marks on the two legs. Using the cordless drill, drill a pilot hole through the marks on each of the legs and into each end of the furring strip.

5. Screw the rung to the legs with one 2" screw in each pilot hole. Repeat for the other four furring strips.

6. Drape your display ladder with blankets, towels, wrapping paper, or whatever else you choose.

05

WORKSPACES, TECHNOLOGY, AND PAPERS

Whether you have a home office or not, wires, papers, and technology are almost certainly part of your daily life. From simple tips on handling cords to setting up a family command center, these hacks will help you make the most of your workspace, no matter how small or large. There's also plenty of tips for organizing craft and hobby supplies, perfect for those creatives out there looking to tame their projects. We'll also dive into the world of paperwork (oh, fun!) and figure out what should stay, what can go, and how to neatly get it all sorted out.

OFFICE ORGANIZATION

When organizing your office, sort all your supplies at once before determining your storage needs. After everything is sorted, assess the best way to store each item and only then should you purchase pieces in which to store them. This will save both time and money and allow you to coordinate your storage containers.

Napkin holders or vintage toast caddies are a stylish way to sort mail or organize small notepads or envelopes.

If you have several projects going at once (or many kids with schedules and important papers to track), create a clipboard wall. Attach clipboards to the wall with nails or adhesive-backed hooks and use each clipboard for a different project, task, or event. Now everyone can instantly see everything that needs to get done.

Make an instant desk by placing two medium-sized filing cabinets spaced apart and lay a flat door across the top. Alternately, you could use two equally sized nightstands with drawers. Now you have a new desk with plenty of room for files or supplies.

If you find yourself missing deadlines or paying bills late, create a spot such as a clipboard or paper tray for "hot" papers and action items. Make it a habit to check it daily.

———

Glue a magnet inside the lid of a mason jar and store paper clips on top. You can fill the mason jar with other supplies such as rubber bands for a one-stop supply shop.

———

Use an old shutter as a way to display cards or memos by sliding or clipping them into the slots.

———

Glam up craft store magnets by gluing pretty rocks, game board pieces, or small trinkets to the top and attach memos or photos to magnet board or refrigerators.

CHIP CANISTER DESK ORGANIZER

While there are various desk sets on the market, it's fun to create one yourself that fits your personal needs. You can mix and match chip canister sizes and yogurt lids to make a desk set for organizing pens, pencils, rulers, scissors, paper clips and sticky notes. The best part is you get to choose the paint color to finish your personalized desk set so that it unequivocally fits your style and decor.

WHAT YOU'LL NEED

2 hot glue sticks

Hot glue gun

2 (5.5-ounce) and 1 (2.5-ounce) chip canisters

1 (3½" × 1") plastic yogurt lid or other metal lid deep enough for paper clips

Thin (4" × 9") wood plaque

Pencil

Newspaper

1 (12-ounce) can spray paint

INSTRUCTIONS

1. Insert a hot glue stick into the hot glue gun and plug it in so it heats up, approximately five minutes. Arrange the canisters and lids on the wooden plaque to see where you would like to place them and trace with a pencil.

2. Put a dab of hot glue on the bottom of each canister and lid and place on the desired spot and apply pressure to adhere, being careful not to have any visible glue or glue strings. Let dry for one minute.

3. Go outside and cover a surface with newspaper to protect from overspray. Spray paint the entire piece using two or three light, even coats with approximately twenty minutes of drying time in between. Let it dry fully for twenty-four hours and then fill it with all your desk supplies for a neat and tidy workspace.

If you have a bookcase and wish to hide the contents so it doesn't look cluttered, attach a roller or roman shade to the front of the bookcase. Roll the shade up to grab supplies then roll it down for clean-looking hidden storage.

Keep track of your schedule by placing a dry erase calendar on the wall. You can use a vinyl wall decal or a dry erase board made for this purpose.

Label the tabs of file folders using a label maker for consistently neat and easy-to-read folder titles.

Remember this golden rule when deciding what to keep on your desk: Desktops should only hold items that are used every day. Store items that are less frequently used out of sight for a neat and efficient workspace.

Add adhesive-backed magnet stickers to the inside bottom of flower-pot saucers and use them to store pushpins and paper clips.

FRAMED DRY ERASE MESSAGE BOARD

There's no need to shell out the big bucks for a boring dry erase board. Make one yourself that fits *your* style! You'll want to choose a light, neutral pattern for the memo area to make notes and daily reminders easier to read. In just five minutes, you'll have a beautiful and handy board to help keep you organized.

WHAT YOU'LL NEED

1 (8" × 10") wall frame, with glass pane

Pencil

1 (8.5" × 11") piece scrapbook paper

Scissors

1 dry erase marker

Dry marker eraser

INSTRUCTIONS

1. Remove the back and the picture mat from the frame, leaving the glass in place. Using the pencil, trace an outline of the outside perimeter of the picture mat onto the back of the scrapbook paper and cut it out with the scissors.

2. Place the paper with the pattern side toward the glass and then replace the mat and the back.

3. Place on your desk and keep your dry erase markers and eraser nearby for whenever you need to jot down a note. Your memo board is ready to go!

ARTS AND CRAFTS SUPPLIES

Turn a shoebox into a ribbon dispenser by cutting small holes evenly along each long side, placing spools inside vertically, and threading the ends of ribbon through the holes so just the ends peek out.

Create a craft station in the inside of a closet with a pegboard, desk, and open shelves for supplies. Hang shoe pockets on the inside of the closet door to create more usable space. The best part is you can close the closet door when finished so the room looks clean and uncluttered.

If you don't have a craft room, use an under-bed storage bin on wheels to contain supplies for easy access.

A shower caddy with a handle works beautifully as a mobile craft station. Fill the caddy with supplies for knitting, crafting, DIY projects, or scrapbooking. Carry it to where you need it, and store it in a cabinet or bookshelf when not in use.

PAINTED DESK SET

No need to spend money on a desk set when you can make a stylish one yourself by transforming mismatched baskets with paint. No matter what they looked like before, a few small baskets in various shapes picked up from thrift stores or yard sales will look like a cohesive set when finished, and you'll have a spot for all your pencils, paper clips, and other office supplies hidden in plain sight.

WHAT YOU'LL NEED

Newspaper

1 (12-ounce) can spray paint

3 small baskets (I used 5" × 5" baskets)

Ruler

Pencil

1 (1.88" × 180') roll painter's tape

1 (2-ounce) bottle craft paint

1 (1") paintbrush

INSTRUCTIONS

1. Go outside and cover a surface with newspaper to protect from overspray. Making sure the baskets are clean of any dust before starting, spray paint the baskets using approximately three light, even coats (with ten minutes drying time in between)

until completely covered. Let the paint dry completely until dry to the touch, about twenty-four hours.

2. On the first basket, use the ruler to measure halfway up from the bottom and draw a faint line around the basket with your pencil. Place a strip of painter's tape above the line and apply all the way around the basket, encircling it. You will paint below that tape. For the second basket, do the same but apply the strip of painter's tape below the line (you will paint above it). For the third basket, apply a strip of painter's tape just below the top edge. Measure one inch below the bottom of the tape and apply a second piece of tape around the basket. You will paint the area between the two pieces of tape.

3. Using the craft paint and paintbrush, completely paint the exposed portion of the baskets. Once it's somewhat dry, about twenty minutes, remove the tape. Don't wait until it's completely dry or you may remove some of the paint. Let the paint dry completely for about twenty-four hours and fill the baskets with office supplies.

10 QUICK WAYS TO ORGANIZE WITH MAGAZINE FILE HOLDERS

Whether you call them magazine holders or file holders, it turns out those ubiquitous boxes can be used to organize just about every space in your home. You can find these made out of cardboard, plastic, or metal, each one with different benefits and drawbacks. Choose the one that best suits your needs. Neutral colors blend in with any decor and don't fall victim to once-trendy patterns that are suddenly out of date. You can even make your own from a cereal box using the Turn a Cereal Box Into a Magazine File tutorial in this chapter. Here are ten ways you can use them to whip various spaces into shape in a few minutes flat:

1. Stack a few sideways in the freezer to increase vertical space for bags of frozen food.

2. Use metal mesh file holders in your pantry to store produce that needs ventilation such as potatoes and onions.

3. Fix one horizontally to the underside of a desk or table for a handy place to hold papers.

4. Mount them sideways under kitchen cabinets to keep boxes of kitchen wrap, aluminum foil, recipes, and zip-top bags handy and off the counters.

5. Put one on a shelf in your closet and place small wallets, clutches, and purses vertically inside.

6. Mount one side to the interior of a cabinet door to store food storage lids, plastic bags, or cleaning products out of the way.

7. Use file holders in the kitchen to organize your cookbooks and recipes. They look much less cluttered when tucked inside the holders and lined up on a shelf.

8. Attach a heatproof one to the side of a bathroom vanity to store styling tools such as curling items, hair dryers, and brushes.

9. Place one horizontally in a corner with the bottom and back against the walls and attach it using small screws and a cordless drill to make a floating shelf with storage inside.

10. A wider file holder works great to stash rolls of toilet paper next to the toilet.

Add corkboard or cork sheets (available in rolls at the craft store) to the inside of an armoire or cabinet doors for a quick place to store memos, fabric scraps, paint swatches, and more.

———

Spool holders are the perfect size for holding rolls of washi tape.

———

Repurpose empty spice jars by filling with glitter or buttons and store them in a spice rack.

———

Utilize the large flat space on top of bookcases and armoires by adding finials vertically to the front edge of the top and store rolls of wrapping paper behind them.

———

If you have a nook or small space between two walls (such as a closet), place a small tension rod inside and thread it with spools of curling ribbon to make a ribbon dispenser.

———

Hang wall-mounted closet or curtain rods in your sewing area and drape with fabric for a pretty wall display. You can also hang small pieces over the top of hanging file folders, one folder per piece of fabric, for a drawer full of organized fabric that can be stored out of sight.

TECHNOLOGY AND CORDS

Add washi tape around a cord toward the plug end and add another piece in the same pattern to its partner. Do this to all your cords using different colors and patterns of washi tape. Now you can match your cords with corresponding electronics in a snap!

———

Plug in a cord and thread the non-plug end through the metal part of a binder clip. Attach it to the side of your furniture so it's at your fingertips and on-duty to charge when needed.

———

Hide cords by bundling them together with Velcro cord holders and attach to adhesive-backed hooks placed strategically along the back of furniture.

———

Toilet paper tubes are a budget-friendly way to store cords and wires when not in use. Fold up cords so they are compact and slide them into toilet paper tubes. Label the tubes and place vertically in a bin for a tangle-free way to find the right cord at the right time.

10 WAYS TO LABEL EVERYTHING

Labels are the icing on the organization cake. Done right, a great label makes any organizer's heart go pitter-patter. Here are ten ways to label just about everything:

1. Vinyl chalkboard labels are great because they can be erased and rewritten on. They even sell tape with a chalkboard-like surface for this purpose. Just neatly cut off a section, write, and label.

2. If you can't find chalkboard labels, make your own. Simply paint wooden tags, available at most craft stores, with chalkboard paint and let it dry for about twenty-four hours before using.

3. Add alphabet stickers to wooden tags for fancy-looking labels.

4. A good label maker is like a best friend: reliable, fun, and makes life better. Use it to label everything from file folders to drawers and shelves to food bins.

5. Use tagboard or kraft tags with twine to neatly label baskets and bins.

6. For large plastic storage totes, make your own protected plastic-coated tags. Type a general label with the contents and print three copies. Slide each copy into a plastic page protector sleeve, and attach to the tote with clear packing tape on three sides of the bin (top, long side, and short side) so you can see what's inside from any direction.

7.   Washi tape makes really pretty labels! Choose a pattern that's not too busy, tear off a section, stick, and then write.

8.   If you have glass containers, get an etching kit and etch the label on the side. This is time intensive to do, but the result can be stunning. This is a wonderful way to label something you plan to have on display.

9.   Take a picture of the contents of a bin and then tape the picture to the front so everyone will know where to put things away. This works also well for shoes, allowing you to quickly see which pairs are in each shoebox.

10. Office supply stores can often laminate labels with sticker paper. Print the labels first and have them laminate them on paper with an adhesive back. You can then easily attach your labels to the bins.

LETTER TRAY CHARGING STATION

Fight messy cords with this DIY charging station that can hold a host of devices while looking stylish and streamlined. Several layers create homes for your devices while the top tray can be used for earphones, speakers, and other important items. This station takes just a few minutes to assemble, so you'll gain control over those cords before they know what hit 'em.

WHAT YOU'LL NEED

Ruler

Pencil

3 (13¼" × 10¼" × 2½") stackable side-loading wooden letter trays

Cordless drill

1" spade drill bit

6-outlet wall tap surge protector

1 package (8) hook and loop cable ties

INSTRUCTIONS

1. With your ruler and pencil, measure and mark where you want the hole for your cords to be placed on two of your trays, approximately 3" in from one side and 1" down from the top (exact measurements will depend on the brand of your letter tray). The third tray should remain free of holes.

2. Using the cordless drill and spade drill bit, drill the holes where you marked them on the back of the two letter trays, clearing sawdust from the hole as you go. Once all holes have been drilled, stack the trays on top of one another with the un-drilled tray on top.

3. Plug your surge protector into an outlet. Plug the cords into the surge protector and run them through the holes in the back of the trays so they can plug into devices. Wrap any excess cord with the hook and loop cable ties to keep the back area neat. Add your accessories to the top tray and enjoy your new charging station.

FILES, PAPERS, AND PHOTOS

When mail comes into your home, open it over the recycling bin. Recycle junk mail before it has a chance to clutter your beautiful home.

While it may sound like a simple step, taking time to set up paperless billing and payments will reduce the amount of mail coming into your home. Be sure to put payment due dates on your calendar for the first billing cycle to make sure all the payments went through smoothly and enjoy the huge amount of paper clutter you're avoiding!

Organize warranties and instruction manuals in expanding folders sorted by room. That way you can always find the right manual simply by searching the folder for that room. Go through it once a year to discard manuals for items you no longer own.

Place all receipts in a magazine file holder. Go through them once a month and discard ones that are no longer needed.

If you pull articles and recipes from magazines, place them in plastic sleeves in a binder or go paperless and upload them so you can save them to *Pinterest* instead.

TURN A CEREAL BOX INTO A MAGAZINE FILE

Cutting cereal boxes is a great way to create upright file holders and storage boxes for students, parents, and busy professionals. Once you cut the cereal box, you can cover it with wrapping paper in whichever pattern your heart desires for a cool and cohesive look.

WHAT YOU'LL NEED

1 (21.6-ounce) family-sized cereal box

Scissors

Ruler

Marker

1 (18" × 30") piece wrapping paper

Pencil

1 (1.4-ounce) extra-strength glue stick

Label

INSTRUCTIONS

1. Cut the top flaps off the cereal box with your scissors so that the top is perfectly straight across on all sides.

2. Use your ruler to measure 5" up from the bottom of the box and mark a line with your marker at this height around the entire box.

3. Using the marker, draw a diagonal line from the top left corner of the wide side of the box down to the line you just drew on the edge of the right-hand side.

4. Turn the box around to the other wide side and draw a diagonal line from the upper right-hand corner down to the line on the edge of the left-hand side.

5. Starting from the top left of the first side, cut down the diagonal line on the front of the box, straight across the line on the skinny side, and back up the line on the other side of the box.

6. Lay the wrapping paper horizontally on a table with the pattern facedown. Lay the box so that one of the large sides is flat on the wrapping paper and the spine of the box is to the right. The left side should be lined up straight with the left side of the wrapping paper, and the bottom edge lined up with the bottom of the wrapping paper. Use a pencil to trace the outline of the top edge of the box, and keeping the right edge firmly on the paper roll the box ninety degrees so that it's on its spine. Continue to trace the top edge so it's connected with the previous line. Repeat this twice more so that the entire box has been traced onto the wrapping paper. Add in an extra inch at the end to create a piece to assist with wrapping in the next step.

7. Measure and draw another line 1" above the entire outline. Cut out the template along this second line using your scissors.

8. Using the glue stick, apply glue over the front of the short, skinny side of the cereal box. Press the non-patterned side of the matching section of wrapping paper onto the glued section of the box, lined up so that the bottom of the paper is flush with the bottom of the box, and smooth out any wrinkles and air bubbles. Note that if lined up correctly there should be 1" of wrapping paper sticking out on the left-hand side and around the top (we will glue this down later).

9. Moving counterclockwise, repeat this process with the large side and the spine.

10. To create a finished look on the last side, you will apply glue to that entire side and first glue down the flap made from the extra inch of wrapping paper you added when making the template. Spread glue with the glue stick on top of that flap so the paper you are about to lay on top will stick to it. Then apply the rest of the wrapping paper over it, making sure to push out any air bubbles or wrinkles, so the flap has been glued down and hidden under that large piece of paper.

11. To finish off the box's top edge, make a cut using the scissors in the exposed wrapping paper at each of the four corners so it folds down easily. Apply glue using the glue stick to the back of the exposed paper, and fold down a section at a time to cover the box's exposed edges. Let it dry for one hour.

12. Add a label on your new file box and place it on a desktop or shelf for an attractive storage solution.

Keep a household inventory for insurance purposes. Take photos of your valuables, everything from clothing to electronics to jewelry, as a record. Keep two copies: one in a fireproof safe in your home and another in a safe-deposit box, in case of loss. Make sure to update this list as valuables are added, sold, or lost.

—————

Keep your grocery list on an app on your phone so you always have it handy and accessible when shopping.

—————

Clear plastic wall pockets are a handy way to hold bills and mail. It's harder to lose them when stored on the wall in front of you as opposed to scattered on your desktop.

—————

If you clip coupons, create a coupon station to keep everything in one easy-to-access area. You'll need a spot for unclipped coupons, a clipped coupon organizer, and scissors.

—————

Create your own coupon organizer by using a small expandable check-sized file. Label each section with a category, such as *dairy*, *produce*, or *frozen*, and file coupons accordingly.

FAMILY AND HOME COMMAND CENTER BINDER

In this busy day and age, it's important to keep track of school papers, phone numbers, information for babysitters, sports schedules, and more. Consider this binder your family playbook and use it to hold all of these items and more. Keep it in one spot where everyone can reference it and you'll never go searching for papers or calendars again.

WHAT YOU'LL NEED

1 (2") three-ring binder with clear plastic cover
Label maker with label tape
1 package (5½" × 11") binder dividers with tabs
Three-hole punch

INSTRUCTIONS

1. Type and print a paper cover labeled "Family Command Center" for your binder and slide it in the clear plastic sheet on the front.

2. Using the label maker, print out the names of the categories you wish to hold in your binder, and then attach them to the binder tabs.

3. Three-hole punch all of your important papers and place them behind the appropriate tab in the binder.

4. Place the binder in one central spot so the entire family can view it quickly and easily.

06

Organizing is a family affair and should be taught to children and incorporated into their routines during their early years so that they may develop effective organization habits for life. Since the organizing needs of kids are in a whole different realm than for adults, this chapter will feature developmentally appropriate hacks and tips that even toddlers can use. Now the entire family can keep toys, stuffed animals, and approximately 78,693 LEGOs under control and easy to find.

KIDS' ROOMS AND TOYS

CLOTHING AND ACCESSORIES

Rolling instead of folding kids' clothing makes it easier to see when storing in drawers. It's especially helpful to roll kids' pajamas together so they have both pieces in one spot.

Corral select items needed for hairstyling, such as detangling spray, a brush, and hair elastics in a portable bin. Sometimes hairstyling happens at the kitchen table a few moments before rushing out the door in the morning, so it's handy to have a "mobile" hair station on hand.

Label a bin designated for outgrown clothing in each kid's closet and toss in clothing as needed. At the end of the season you'll have all of your clothing to donate, hand down, or resell in one spot.

Update an old dresser by painting the front of the drawers with chalkboard paint and label the drawer fronts with what's inside so kids know where to find shirts, pants, and socks.

CUSTOMIZED KIDS' CLOSET

Kids' closets can quickly become havens for sprawling messes. Creating a customized and easily organized closet helps teach kids good organizing systems that develop into strong habits. This system also empowers kids to start dressing themselves at an early age since everything is laid out for them. All in all, this customized kids' closet helps make everybody's life easier!

WHAT YOU'LL NEED

1 box trash bags

1 box cleaning wipes

Vacuum

1 double hang closet rod

Child-sized hangers

1 (36" tall) 5-shelf hanging closet organizer

Label maker with label tape

Cordless drill with driver bit

2 (2") screws

Wall mount Shaker wood peg rack with 6 pegs

4 medium adhesive-backed hooks

1 (30-gallon) plastic storage tote

Hamper

INSTRUCTIONS

1. Remove all items from the closet, sorting them into three piles as you go: Keep, Outgrown, and Trash (the Trash pile should go into a trash bag). Clean the closet with cleaning wipes and vacuum the floor.

2. Hang the double hang rod from the already installed clothing rod. Hang out-of-season or infrequently used clothing on child-sized hangers along the top closet rod and hang the current season's clothing on the double hang rod.

3. Hang the closet organizer next to the section with the double hang rod. Use the label maker and label tape to label each shelf with a weekday for easy school-day dressing. Either you or your child can then pull out five outfits from the bottom bar, one for each weekday, and fill each hanging shelf with an outfit.

4. Using the cordless drill and the 2" screws, attach the wood peg rack to the back of the closet a few inches off the floor but below the clothes on the bottom bar so they're still visible to match with each day's outfit. Kids can place a shoe onto each hook so they're stored off the floor yet easily accessible.

5. Stick adhesive-backed hooks on the sides of the closet next to the closet organizer and just below the double hang rod. Hang hats, bags of supplies, costumes, or other accessories so your child can accessorize each day's outfit and make it his or her own.

6. Label the plastic bin "Outgrown Clothes" and place it on a top shelf above the clothes. As soon as something is too small, pop it in the bin. At the end of the season donate everything in the bin to a worthy charity, hand it down to a younger sibling or cousin, or store for future kiddos.

7. Finalize your new and improved custom closet with a place to drop dirty clothes by placing a hamper inside. Now you have a clean and easily organized closet to help your kids get ready every morning!

TOYS

· · · · · · · ·

Keep doll outfits organized by placing them in zip-top bags and lining them up in a box or small bin.

———

Purchase half-wall planter baskets at the home improvement or garden store. Using wall anchors, mount them to the wall in groups for attractive (and out-of-the-way) toy storage.

———

Place doll outfits in sturdy plastic pockets in a large binder for an easy doll wardrobe.

———

Avoid the dreaded pain of stepping on a LEGO by using a fitted sheet as a space for LEGO play. When kids are done, pull up the corners and store out of the way until inspiration strikes again.

———

When storing outgrown shoes to hand down to younger brothers and sisters, label large zip-top bags with the size and type of footwear and fill. Then, stack the bags in large bins labeled "shoes" so whenever you need the next size up, you can find it instantly.

If you live in a home with multiple levels, have two baskets for collecting items. One should be placed downstairs with items that need to go upstairs and vice versa. At the end of the day, make it a habit to bring one up and the other down and have the kids put everything away in the appropriate place.

———

Make sorting and storing toys easy for nonreaders by using clear plastic bins so everyone can see the contents inside.

———

Use adhesive-backed hooks attached to the wall sideways to hold taut the ends of a piece of plastic chain. Clip stuffed animals or other soft small toys to the chain for cute wall storage.

———

Place painter's tape on the floor of the garage to designate "parking spots" for ride-on toys and bikes and watch your kids properly put away their toys in their new makeshift parking lot.

———

Make a LEGO brick wall at home by using plastic hexagonal candy jars, which allow the bricks to sit inside and not fall out. Attach a jar to the wall by the bottom so the opening is facing out. Fill each jar with bricks sorted by color. Now kids can "pick a brick" at home and you have a cool new feature wall.

EASY UNDER-BED STORAGE ON WHEELS

While under-bed storage bins are a fantastic way to use the large space available under beds, accessing them can often be unwieldy. This is an easy way to add wheels to the bottom, which makes pulling them out and tucking them away a breeze. Kids especially love these wheeled drawers as ways to store toys that require a flat space to work. Plus, this project repurposes old drawers, which makes them a breeze to quickly put together.

WHAT YOU'LL NEED

Dresser drawer with handles (approximately 30" long × 16" wide)

Ruler

Pencil

Cordless drill

16 (½") screws

4 (2") standard casters with swivel plate

INSTRUCTIONS

1. Flip the dresser drawer facedown so that the bottom is exposed. With your ruler, measure about 1¼" out from each side of all corners and use your pencil to mark where you will attach the casters.

2. With the cordless drill, using one screw in each of the four corners of the caster, screw the casters into the outside bottom of the drawer. If the screws poke through the bottom of the drawer, a piece of foam core cut to fit the entire inside of the drawer can safely and attractively cover them.

3. Load up any toys or out-of-season clothes and slide it under the bed for easily accessible storage.

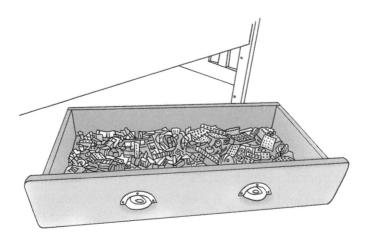

Attach buckets with handles to hooks mounted on the wall for cute and handy toy storage. Kids can take them down, play, clean up, and rehang when finished.

———

Make a garage for toy cars by gluing sections of PVC pipe onto a board. Mount the board to the wall and slide the cars into each pipe for a "parking garage" to help kids tidy up their toys.

———

Zippered mesh or clear plastic pencil pouches from a dollar store are great for storing puzzle pieces or sets of small toys. If the pouches have three holes, clip them in a labeled binder and line them all up on a shelf.

———

Keep your dollhouse accessories sorted by purchasing a few sets of flat plastic drawers and placing the dollhouse on top. Secure the dollhouse to the wall with furniture safety straps to prevent tipping. Now you can store everything in the plastic drawers under the dollhouse.

———

Costumes for playing dress-up can easily get out of control. Take the shelves out of a bookcase and add a clothing rod toward the top along with a mirror on the side to transform it into a costume wardrobe. Baskets placed on the bottom are the perfect place to store accessories and shoes, and hooks along the other side are great for scarves, boas, and hats.

DOLLAR STORE STORAGE JARS

Kids go wild for these cute and clever jars that are perfect for storing small toys. They look especially great when lined up together on a shelf and make it easy to "grab and go" favorite toy collections for road trips or moving from room to room. Once you get started making them, you'll find that it's hard to stop; you're sure to find many uses for these smile-inducing jars around your home!

WHAT YOU'LL NEED

Hot glue gun

2 hot glue sticks

Items to place on lids (plastic animals, game pieces, seashells, small toys, etc.)

5 (38-ounce) plastic jars with lids

Newspaper

1 (12-ounce) can spray paint

INSTRUCTIONS

1. Insert a hot glue stick into the hot glue gun and plug it in so it heats up, approximately five minutes. Place the object of your choice on the lid of the jar and use the hot glue gun to attach it with a dab of glue in the correct spot. Be sure that the glue is not visible or else the glue will show once you spray paint it. Let it dry for five minutes.

2. Go outside and cover a surface with newspaper to protect from overspray. Spray paint the lids using two or three light, even coats until totally covered. Let dry completely, about twenty-four hours.

3. Fill the jars with objects similar to what you placed on the lid, such as plastic dinosaurs in the jar with the T. rex on top, and screw the lids into place. Line them all up on a shelf and enjoy.

ART, BOOKS, AND GAMES

Use a plastic file box to gather all of your kids' art projects in one spot, and go through it periodically to save your favorites.

An ordinary plastic caddy or wheeled storage cart transforms into a mobile art station when filled with crayons, markers, and glue sticks. Add a hook on the side to hang a smock or small apron. This makes it easy to create art on the go, whenever the mood strikes.

Plastic baby wipes containers make excellent crayon and marker boxes once they are emptied and cleaned.

Paint the top of a small table with chalkboard paint for a custom art table kids will love. Place a bucket of chalk on top and let them create masterpieces that they can erase and redraw again and again.

Make a portable art caddy by securing a tool belt or tool apron around the outside of a large bucket from the home improvement store. Use the inside of the bucket to store paper and bulky crafting items and use the pockets of the belt for smaller supplies such as markers and tape.

10 WAYS TO ORGANIZE AND DISPLAY KIDS' ART

Kids' artwork can multiply exponentially, especially in the preschool years when they seem to come home with a new (and possibly noodle-filled) project each day. It's hard to part with these precious early examples of artistic genius. However, keeping everything isn't always possible due to space issues. Here are ten ways to handle honoring kids' art without having to wallpaper your living room with it.

1. Clotheslines are a fun way to display art. The plus side is that art is easy to change with a quick snap of the clothespin or clip.

2. Purchase several large picture frames and remove the glass. Glue a clothespin inside the frame. Now you have open space to clip art in and out as it comes home.

3. Get a particularly inspired piece printed on mugs, pillowcases, or even a T-shirt or blanket! There are many online photo printing stores that offer this service.

4. You can upload and print drawings and paintings onto a wrapped canvas. This gives the art permanence and can be passed down when your kids have homes of their own.

5. If you have a playroom or craft room, line one of the walls with corkboard. This fun wall treatment makes it a cinch to rearrange art on a whim.

6. Magnetic chalkboard paint works for hanging art as well. You can get it tinted to whatever color you'd like, and then use magnets to attach the art. Draw frames around them in chalk to really make the art stand out.

7. If you have art that you don't plan to keep but don't want to throw it in the trash, use it as gift wrap for family members. They'll enjoy seeing the pictures but no one is obligated to keep it.

8. Have pieces of clear acrylic plastic cut to size and use them as floating frames. Drive pilot holes in all four corners of the acrylic. Lightly attach the art to the wall using a nonpermanent adhesive (like a picture hanging strip), place the piece of acrylic on top, and screw it into the wall at all four corners.

9. For the really special pieces you wish to save, purchase an artist's portfolio and use it to collect your favorites over the years.

10. Use an app such as Artkive to photograph the art and store it online. You can then recycle the actual paper knowing the masterpiece can be reprinted if needed.

If you have babies or toddlers, store board books in a basket to make them easy to grab and put away. You can worry about shelving them properly when the children get a bit older but, for now, enjoy the ease of book baskets.

———

Give coloring books their own home by creating coloring stations. Store them in a clear bin with a flat top and tuck a pencil box full of crayons inside. You now have a DIY coloring station at your fingertips.

———

Store holiday books in bins by season. At the start of each season or holiday, put them out where kids can enjoy them, perhaps in a special basket for seasonal books, and put last season's bin into storage.

———

Most picture books come with paper covers that are easily ripped or destroyed. Stop the madness before it starts and take the paper covers off and store in a safe place until kids are older. Books will look like new when you slide the paper covers back on.

———

Card games often seem to outlive their boxes. Plastic diaper wipes containers make an excellent replacement. Fill cleaned and dried containers with the cards, attach the cover of the old box to the side of the new one, and stack.

Store puzzles in mesh sports bags or inexpensive drawstring bags. Tie on a tag that labels the contents and line the bags up on a shelf or hang from hooks. Just be sure to include a photo of the finished puzzle so you know what you're making as you put it together.

Store board games in plain sight by framing them and taping zip-top bags with game pieces to the back. Hang them on the wall for storage that doubles as decor.

Using hanging sweater shelves to store board games enables you to easily see the titles. This handy hack means you'll have no more teetering towers of flimsy boxes while you're trying decide what to play.

Make a temporary gallery wall that can be easily changed by using washi tape to secure kids' art to the walls. You may wish to make a color photocopy of the original art so the tape doesn't damage it, then create frames with washi tape around each masterpiece. To change the gallery, simply remove the tape and hang up new works of art!

TANK TOP TURNED TOY STORAGE TOTE

This quick trick will turn any tank top into a market-style bag that's perfect for storing toys or really anything that you would like to gather and hold together. You can use an old tank top from the discards in your closet, find one at a thrift store, or buy a new (inexpensive) one. You can even use a T-shirt and cut off the sleeves to make a tank.

WHAT YOU'LL NEED

Adult medium-sized tank top, washed and dried

10 sewing pins

1 needle

2 (20") pieces of thread

INSTRUCTIONS

1. Start by turning the tank top inside out.

2. Pin the fabric together in a straight line across the bottom.

3. Thread the needle with one of the pieces of thread and tie a knot at the end. Using the needle and thread and starting ½" from the bottom, sew straight across the bottom then tie it off. Repeat this step immediately below the first seam with the second piece of thread to create a strong bond.

4. Turn it right side out and fill it with toys.

BABIES AND PRESCHOOLERS

When you have a baby, diaper changes happen often and just about everywhere. Place diapering supplies such as diapers, cream, a changing pad, and wipes in a handled caddy and put it in an inconspicuous place. Your mobile caddy will really come in handy when the inevitable need strikes.

Use an adhesive-backed hook to attach clean bibs to the back of a high chair for convenient storage that takes up very little space.

Ditch the changing table and invest in a sturdy dresser topped with a safe changing pad instead. After the diaper stage, the dresser can be used for years to come.

MARKER STORAGE FOR LITTLE ARTISTS

Trying to keep the caps on markers with young children around is a nightmare. Caps always seem to roll away and markers dry out because they are improperly closed. This project makes it easy to match the caps and markers and ensure all are capped correctly. When a marker eventually dries out, simply add a new one in the old space and toss the new cap and old marker.

WHAT YOU'LL NEED

1 pack (10) washable kids' markers

Ruler

1 (9" × 5") loaf pan

1 (1.88" × 180') roll painter's tape

Newspaper

3 cups Plaster of Paris

3 cups water

1 (48-ounce) disposable plastic container

1 wooden stirring stick

Timer

INSTRUCTIONS

1. Take the markers out of the box and take the caps off and on a few times to loosen them up. Once they set in the plaster, you don't want to wiggle them much.

2. Using the ruler, measure up 1¼" from the bottom of the loaf pan and mark this spot with tape. This is the mark for how high you should pour the Plaster of Paris.

3. Protect your workspace by laying down newspaper. Follow the package instructions for mixing the Plaster of Paris with water, using the disposable container and stirring stick. Carefully pour the Plaster of Paris into the loaf pan, making sure not to go over the taped area.

4. Let the plaster harden slightly, approximately fifteen to thirty minutes. You'll want the plaster soft enough to push the markers into the plaster but not so soft that they fall over. Set a timer to check every five minutes within this range until it's just right.

5. Once the consistency is right, push the markers cap-side first into the plaster. It should be firm enough to hold them perfectly upright.

6. Let dry completely according to package directions. The plaster should be completely set; otherwise the marker caps will come loose. Once dry, your marker holder is ready for use!

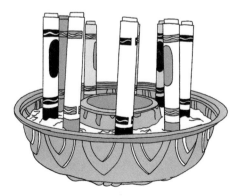

10 USES FOR ADHESIVE-BACKED HOOKS

If there were a hall of fame of organizing products, adhesive-backed hooks would be among the elite. First and foremost, they are removable, which makes them an easy way to hang items without nail holes. They are available in various colors, including metallic tones that look higher-end, and you can find sizes ranging from micro to ginormous.

1. Attach hooks to the inside of your shower wall and use as a spot to drip-dry bathing suits.

2. Create a "hat wall" in your closet using small adhesive-backed hooks to hang caps.

3. Place them on a wall in your closet for a beautiful and colorful way to display all your scarves.

4. Belt buckles loop perfectly on the metal adhesive-backed hooks.

5. Stick two per lid to the inside of your kitchen cabinets to store pot and pan lids.

6. Never lose your keys again when you stick a few small hooks by the door and habitually place keys on them each time you walk in.

7. Create a pet station with leashes and waste disposal bags clipped onto hooks by the door.

8. Tuck a few dish towels on hooks on the side of your kitchen island.

9. Place a few hooks on the inside of your pantry door to hang aprons.

10. Hang silicone potholders within reach near, but not over, the stove and you'll never accidentally grab a hot pan by mistake again.

Pack school lunches the night before and place them in the fridge. Kids can help and will enjoy having more choice in what they're eating for lunch. In the morning, add an ice pack and they're ready to go.

————

Showcase toy collections as decor and make tidying methods a game to show kids that storage and organization can be fun!

————

When decluttering toys, ask your kids to find toys that are "babyish" to hand down or donate. Often they'll want to purge "baby" toys so this wording works like a charm.

————

Involve kids in helping you sort and label bins so they feel they have ownership in the process. They'll be more invested in upkeep this way.

07

Laundry rooms, garages, attics, and basements are multi-tasking rooms that handle many jobs. This heavy use adds up, and as a result these areas can look worse for the wear. These tips and hacks will help these spaces run as efficiently as possible while keeping everything tidy and organized. Laundry might even become a new favorite hobby.

UTILITY AND STORAGE SPACES

LAUNDRY ROOM

· ·

It's hard to keep track of which items aren't supposed to go in the dryer. Keep those items safe by placing them inside a mesh bag in the washing machine. When the load is finished, pull that bag out first and air-dry the items instead.

———

If you have a white or light-colored washing machine, stick a magnetic dry erase marker on the lid. When you toss items into the washer, use the dry erase marker to write reminder notes such as which items needed to be double-checked for stains or which items can't go in the dryer. Wipe off and repeat with the next load.

———

Purchase a wall-mounted drying rack for your laundry room and you'll have a spot to air-dry items that can be tucked out of the way when not in use.

———

A retractable wall-mounted drying line provides a spot to hang clothing, and you can snap it out of the way in an instant between loads.

Find space to hang a closet rod in your laundry room. Being able to hang clothes right out of the dryer means less wrinkles.

———

If you have a front-loading washing machine, build a simple counter above it for folding and storage. You can do this by anchoring two braces to the walls on either side of the washer and dryer and attaching a piece of wood cut to size over the top, making sure there's enough room for proper ventilation.

———

Mount two large hooks to the wall and hang your ironing board on them in style.

———

Pour liquid laundry detergent into a glass beverage dispenser and hang the spigot over the side of a shelf. It looks pretty, makes it easy to dispense detergent, and you'll always see when you need more.

———

Hang a towel bar under a shelf above the washer and dryer to use as a clothing rod for hanging clothes.

LOST SOCK SIGN

Streamline laundry day with a lost sock sign and collection area. By clipping single socks onto the sign, you'll never have to wonder where their partners are again because you'll be able to match them with their previously lonely "sole" mates in mere seconds flat.

WHAT YOU'LL NEED

1 sheet fine grade sandpaper

1 (18½" × 6½") wooden board

1 (18" × 36") tack cloth

Newspaper

2 (12-ounce) cans spray paint, two colors

5 clothespins

1 cardboard box, any size

Hot glue gun

2 hot glue sticks

2 large (2½") sawtooth picture hangers with nails

Hammer

Ruler

Pencil

1 pack medium-sized alphabet stickers

Level

2 (1½") nails

INSTRUCTIONS

1. Sand the wooden board with the sandpaper until smooth and wipe away sawdust using the tack cloth.

2. Go outside and cover a surface with newspaper to protect from overspray, then spray paint the board with three light, even coats of paint, letting them dry about ten minutes in between.

3. Clip the clothespins to the side of the cardboard box to easily reach every angle, and spray with two or three even coats of spray paint until fully covered. Let dry completely until dry to the touch, about twenty-four hours.

4. Insert a hot glue stick into the hot glue gun and plug it in so it heats up, approximately five minutes. Attach the sawtooth hangers to the back of the board, one in each of the top corners ½" from the top and each side, by hammering in the small nails that came in the package.

5. Use the ruler to measure 5" up from the bottom on the front of the board, then draw a horizontal line with your pencil across the board. Every 3" along this line, make a mark to note where the clothespins should go. Using the hot glue gun, attach the clothespins (one on each mark) with the clip ends facing downward and apply light pressure to help them adhere. Let each dry one minute before advancing to the next.

6. Draw a line with your pencil where you would like the letters to be attached, using a ruler to make sure everything stays straight. Arrange the letters while the backing is still on to figure out the spacing needed, then peel the back paper off the sticker and push each letter down in its spot so it's firmly attached.

7. Find the center of your sawtooth hangers on the back of your sign and make a faint mark with your pencil on the top of your sign in each of those spots. Hold your sign up on the wall where you would like it to hang. Use a level to make sure it's straight, then mark the wall at those two spots with your pencil. Use your ruler to measure 1" down from each of those marks and hammer a nail at those spots so the end is protruding far enough from the wall to hang your sign.

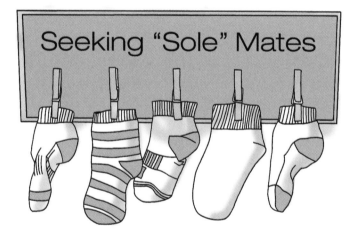

Many laundry rooms are equipped with wire shelving. Make the shelves work harder by attaching S-hooks to the underside of them. Hang cleaning tools from the hooks to make use of every inch of space.

———

Create a laundry room "stain station" by placing tools such as a bleach pen, stain gel, and a small brush on a lazy Susan. Spin the wheel and grab what you need!

———

Label each section of your laundry sorter with the type of wash it should contain. This way the entire family knows exactly where to put dirty clothing.

———

Place containers to assist with frequently repeated tasks on a shelf in your laundry room. These might include a bin for items to be repaired, a container for coins, a caddy with items to treat stains, and a box for lost socks.

———

Have a designated spot for items to use for clothing repair, such as scissors, thread, needle, and patches so they're easy to find.

10 WAYS TO USE TRASH CANS OTHER THAN FOR TRASH

Trash cans are an inexpensive way to store bulky items. They come in various sizes and materials and can be found for as little as a dollar at many retailers. You can use trash cans in ways you may never have imagined, as you will see in this list:

1. Potting soil can get messy. Keep it neatly contained in a small trash can with a lid.

2. If you live in a climate that experiences winter, you're no stranger to rock salt. A small lidded trash can with rock salt keeps it out of the way yet handy when winter weather hits.

3. A decorative trash can with a wide, flat bottom becomes a handy side table when inverted.

4. Metal trash cans are great storage spots for rolls of wrapping paper.

5. A medium-sized trash can doubles well as an umbrella stand near the entryway or in a mudroom.

6. Christmas garlands or outdoor decorations can be stored in large lidded trash cans for a way to keep them dust-free and protected.

7. Turn a trash can into a compost bin. Poke holes in the side so the compost has air to decompose and use this bin as a place to collect your food scraps and yard waste that you can turn into rich soil.

8. Place a small trash bin in your laundry room out of the way but near the dryer. This makes for a handy spot to dispose of lint and used dryer sheets without making a big mess.

9. Place several small trash cans side by side to create an organized station in which to sort your recycling.

10. If you are a DIYer and have scrap pieces of lumber, store them in a trash can upright and out of the way.

Create a clever drying rack inside a spare drawer in your laundry room. Take the bottom off the drawer and attach a rod inside. When you need to air-dry or hang something, pull out the drawer and use the hidden drying space below.

———

Socks in various colors and patterns are fun, but consider purchasing packs of the same colored socks in bulk to make matching a cinch. Designate one pattern/color per person in your household and you'll find that putting them away takes less time because you'll instantly be able to match them together and know to whom they belong.

———

If you use your laundry room as a place to store cleaning supplies, put them in a caddy with a handle so you'll be able to tote them from room to room. Having all your cleaning materials in one spot saves time, money, and space.

GARAGE

· · · · · · · · · · · ·

Keep pet food in sealed containers such as big popcorn tins or small lidded trash cans, possibly with a bungee cord to secure the top if you have a wily pet.

———

Make a donation bin part of the landscape in your garage. Whenever you come across an item to donate, place it in the bin. When it gets full, it's time for a trip to the thrift store.

———

Keep your home's color palette handy by painting one end of a wooden tongue depressor each room's color. Once dry, label each tongue depressor with the paint brand, color, and room. Drill a hole in the other end and attach to a binder ring to create on-the-go home color swatches.

———

Keep small amounts of touch-up paint on hand by storing it in baby food jars. Place a piece of plastic wrap between the lid and the paint to create a seal so it doesn't dry out.

Repurpose a dresser by turning it into a workbench. The drawers can contain hardware and tools, and the top can be used as a workspace.

———

If you have leftover paint, decant it into smaller cans from a home improvement store. Add new labels with the paint brand, color formula, date, and room. This takes a little extra work but will be worth it to reduce the amount of space needed for your paint collection. Plus this makes your paint supplies look much tidier and cohesive.

ALL-IN-ONE MASON JAR HARDWARE STORAGE AND TWINE DISPENSER

Consider this a blueprint for a hardworking hardware station that maximizes storage space in your workshop or craft room beautifully. It's flexible too; you don't have to include the twine dispenser if that's not a need or you can use smaller jars for under the shelf if you only have small hardware to store. Instead of nuts and bolts, you can use this hack for rice and beans in a kitchen, or washi tape and ribbon in a craft room. Mason jars are ready to serve your needs in one handy spot regardless of where or how you use them.

WHAT YOU'LL NEED

1 (23" × 7" × 6½") wooden shelf with notches on the back for hanging

3 (quart-sized) mason jars

2 (pint-sized) mason jars

Ruler

Pencil

Protected workspace such as a workbench or table
with a piece of scrap lumber on top

Protective eyewear

Hammer

1 (3" 10D) nail

Cordless drill with driver bit

1 (³⁄₁₆") *drill bit*

15 (¾") *screws*

1 (2") *nail*

2 rolls (5" height × 2" diameter) *twine*

Level

2 (1¼") *wall anchors with screws*

INSTRUCTIONS

1. Flip the wooden shelf over so the underside is facing up and take the lids off all of the jars. Using the ruler, measure 3½" in from the long sides and, using a pencil, draw a line horizontally down the middle. Use your ruler and pencil to measure and mark three spots along this line at 6½" from the edge, 11½", and 16½", then place the three quart-sized mason jar lids on these spots. Use the pencil to trace the lids and remove.

2. Place a lid bottom side up on a protected workspace or piece of scrap lumber. Wearing your protective eyewear, hammer the smaller nail through the back side of the lid in three evenly spaced and separate areas toward the edge of the lid to create your screw holes. Do this with all five lids.

3. Place the quart-sized lids onto the bottom of the shelf again inside the previously traced circles. Make a mark on the wood with your pencil through each screw hole and remove lids. Using the cordless drill, drill a pilot hole using the ³⁄₁₆" drill bit into each space. Place the quart-sized lids back on and use the driver bit in your drill and the screws to attach the lids into place. You'll want to make sure the screws are firmly attached

but not so tight that they buckle the metal of the lid. Screw the mason jars into their lids and flip the shelf so it is now right side up with the mason jars underneath.

4. Measure 3½" in toward the middle from the long edge and draw a line down the center of the length of your shelf. Place the two pint-sized mason jars upside down along it. You will want to place these jars in the gaps between the three jars below (approximately 9" in from each side) to leave room for your twine to hang. Trace the two jar lids onto the shelf using the pencil and then remove the jars.

5. Using a large drill bit, drill a hole large enough for the twine to fit through in the center of each traced circle on the top of the shelf.

6. Place the two remaining mason jar lids with the bottoms up, one in each circle. Use the hammer and larger nail to punch a hole in the center of each lid that is large enough for the twine to fit.

7. Make a mark with your pencil through each of the outer screw holes onto the wood and remove lids. You will not be screwing into the center holes, so don't mark them. Drill pilot holes at these marks, replace lids (again, bottom side up), and screw onto the shelf at each of the screw holes in the lids. Attach screws so each lid is firmly but not too tightly mounted onto the shelf. Fill the two top jars with twine, thread it through the center holes in both the lids and the shelf, and screw the jars into the lids.

8. Remove the jars before you hang the shelf. Place the shelf where you would like it on the wall, then use the level to make sure it's straight and draw a light line across the top in pencil. Measure where the notches are on the back of your shelf using your ruler, and measure and mark the matching location on the line on your wall so you know where to place the wall anchors. Following the instructions your package of wall anchors, securely attach them to the wall in the spaces you marked, with the head of the screws protruding slightly to hang on the notches. Hang the shelf on the screws, fill and screw jars onto the shelf, and get ready for maximum efficiency the next time you need hardware or twine!

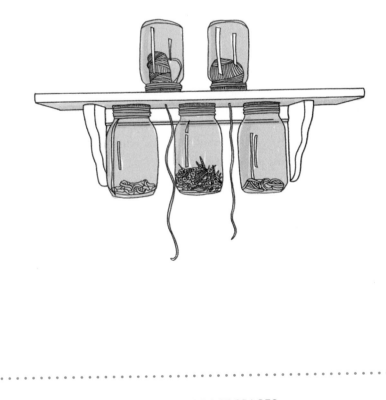

Give plain old tools new life by dipping the handles in a plastic coating dip. Give all your tools this makeover and they'll look like a brand new set.

———

Adhere heavy duty magnets to the side of a flashlight, and attach to your breaker panel. In case of a blown fuse or tripped circuit, you'll know exactly where the flashlight is located and be able to easily see if you need to fix it.

———

Store small hardware such as nails and screws in bead organizers by size and category.

———

Paint pegboards a favorite color, add stripes, or even paint on your last initial. Frame it with molding and you'll be the envy of the neighborhood.

———

Screw the bottom of a large bucket into a wall and coil your garden hose around it. Use the opening of the bucket to store the sprayer and sponges.

———

Attach a magnetic knife strip to the side of your workbench or the wall above and use it to hold drill bits.

(10) PLACES TO USE A PEGBOARD

Pegboards have been used for organizing for a while now, but they were traditionally relegated to garages. However, these task masters can be used to organize almost any space and decorated to fit in just about everywhere. For full instructions on how to properly hang a pegboard, follow the How to Hang a Pegboard tutorial later in this chapter, but for now, check out all the many ways to use one:

1. A pegboard in your office can hold desk supplies, calendars, memo boards, wall pockets, and more. Put it on the wall above your desk and enjoy a clean surface with your supplies within reach.

2. From a pegboard, use hooks to hang various-sized buckets in a kid's room to store small toys and stuffed animals. Hooks are also great for hanging hoodies. Paint the pegboard a bold color or with the child's initial to make it a focal point of the room's decor.

3. Utility areas such as laundry rooms and mudrooms are perfect places for pegboards. Use them to hang cleaning supplies such as dusters, rags, lint rollers, and brooms. A pegboard makes even your basic supplies look great.

4. Follow the lead of culinary legend Julia Child, who famously not only used pegboards to hold cooking equipment in her kitchen but also outlined each piece on the board so everyone knew exactly what to put where.

5. If you do use a pegboard in the kitchen for utensils and pots and pans, don't forget the lids. Pegboard hooks are the perfect way to hang those bulky and difficult-to-store items.

6. Craft rooms are pegboard nirvana. Small buckets hanging from a pegboard can hold scissors and coloring supplies, larger hanging trays are perfect for corralling glitter and small jars, and hooks are great for hanging ribbon and tape. You can even mount small crates using extended hooks (with their opening facing out) and fill them with craft paint.

7. Photo galleries can take hours to plan and perfectly install, so for a fun take try them on a pegboard. You can move the hooks around and quickly rearrange art and photos, making installation and alterations a breeze.

8. Technology accessories such as remotes, headphones, and gaming equipment tend to overtake living spaces and playrooms. Install a pegboard and hang them up instead. Hanging buckets work well for remotes and you can also install larger boxes to hold DVD and Blu-ray discs or video game cases. When organizing becomes intentional, even electronics can be stored beautifully.

9. Bathrooms are often short on space. Hang a small pegboard and use it to hold hair dryers, curling irons, and brushes. If there's room, you can also add hooks for jewelry to create a one-stop shop full of supplies to get you ready in the morning.

10. And, yes, you can still use pegboards in your garage. They really are an effective way to organize power tools and hardware, and the hooks come in many varieties for this very purpose.

Try this inexpensive and easy solution for storing fishing rods. Attach two pool noodles horizontally to a garage wall, one on the floor and one two to three feet up. Cut vertical slits into the top pool noodle in regular intervals and matching slots in the bottom noodle. Place the handle into the bottom noodle and nestle the middle of the rod in the vertical slit above. Fishing rods will nestle safely in their new pool noodle home.

———

Make a wall-mounted screwdriver holder by drilling equally spaced holes through the wood of a small shelf, mounting it to the wall, and inserting screwdrivers tip down through the holes.

———

If you have open studs in your garage, use those nooks to add shelving, hooks, and bungees to hold sports equipment in between.

———

Use a large-wheeled garbage can to hold tall gardening tools and lawn-care supplies. Store away when not in use and wheel it to where it's needed when working in the yard.

Use a plastic box with compartments to organize your batteries by size. No more struggling to open packages or running out of AAAs right when you need them!

If you use your garage for storage, make it easy to find what you need and give it a cohesive look by investing in plastic storage bins of the same size and color. Place bins on industrial shelves along the wall and label each bin neatly with its contents. Put less-often used items toward the top and frequently needed things within easy reach.

A rolling laundry sorter makes a great storage piece for sports and playground equipment since it can be moved as needed and has plenty of room for oddly shaped equipment.

HOW TO HANG A PEGBOARD

Pegboards are the epitome of organization bliss. You can configure them thousands of different ways and use them in almost any room. Before you start, measure the area where you plan to hang the pegboard. We're going to use a 4' × 4' pegboard. If that doesn't fit, most home improvement stores can cut it to size. You will also need a partner to hold it up while you secure it to the wall, so call up that friend or neighbor who owes you a favor.

WHAT YOU'LL NEED

Stud finder

Pencil

2 (1" × 2" × 48") furring strips

Level

Cordless drill with driver bit

32 (2") screws

3 (1" × 2" × 44") furring strips

1 (4' × 4') pegboard

INSTRUCTIONS

1. Use the stud finder to locate studs near where you wish to hang the pegboard and mark the stud locations with a pencil. Have your partner hold one of the 48" furring strips horizontally against the wall at the top of where you'd like the pegboard to hang and over the studs.

2. Use the level to make sure it's straight and draw a line on the wall so you know where it should be placed in case it shifts when drilling.

3. Using the cordless drill, drill pilot holes through the furring strip into the studs every 16", and attach it to the wall using the screws. Repeat this process for the bottom furring strip, mounting the other 48" furring strip horizontally in the same way so it sits 46" below the bottom of the top strip. Then mount your three shorter furring strips vertically on the studs following the same method; two should be on either end to create a frame and one down the middle. Secure each strip with three screws drilled right into the studs. The furring strips will be hidden by the pegboard once it's mounted in the next step.

4. Have your partner hold the pegboard over the frame. Use the level to make sure it's straight. Use the cordless drill with driver bit to attach it to the furring strip frame with the remaining fifteen screws evenly spaced around the edges.

ATTIC AND BASEMENT

When storing items, keep in mind papers, photos, candles, and electronics should never be stored in the attic due to the potential for melting in the heat or infestation from critters.

Build shelves between attic trusses to utilize hidden space and keep the floor free from clutter. This can be as easy as adding a piece of plywood on top of support beams between trusses, or attach it to the trusses themselves about halfway up.

Basements are a haven for moisture. Avoid storing heirlooms, art, or photographs in this space. Use plastic bins to protect from dampness and store these types of items under beds in your home instead.

Store items in your basement off the floor in case of flooding. Even an inch of water can do a whole lot of damage when wood, paper, and metal are involved.

If you have items in storage bins, keeping an inventory can be helpful. Label each bin with a number and keep an inventory list with the numbers and the contents in a handy spot.

BEHIND-THE-DOOR WRAPPING STATION

While there are many options for organizing wrapping supplies, this one using shoe pockets is particularly wonderful. Everything is organized in one small and easy-to-reach space, and there is no need to haul out containers from under beds or inside closets. Another bonus is you can see exactly what you have to choose from.

WHAT YOU'LL NEED

1 (24-pocket) shoe pocket organizer
1 (12" × 18") cutting mat
Utility knife

INSTRUCTIONS

1. Laying the shoe pocket organizer on the cutting mat, locate the second row of shoe pockets from the bottom.

2. Use the utility knife to carefully cut through the plastic just above the seam at the bottom of each of the pockets in this row, making sure not to cut through the back layer. Repeat this for the third row from the bottom.

3. Hang the wrapping paper organizer behind a door using the hooks that came in the package and slide wrapping paper rolls through the newly created sleeves so they nest inside the bottom pockets.

4. Fill the remaining pockets with tape, scissors, ribbon, and gift tags so you're ready to wrap.

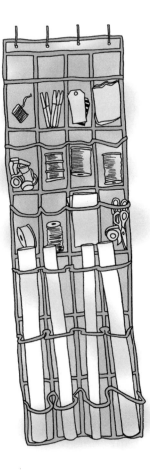

08

Because the unexpected happens on the go, these tips will help make traveling, organizing your car, and even moving as stress-free as possible. Changing seasons also brings unique organization challenges, so you'll find plenty of seasonal organizing tips here, including how to store holiday decorations and handle summer clutter.

EVERYTHING ELSE

TRAVEL

· · · · · · · · · · ·

Place disposable shower caps around the bottoms of shoes to separate them from the rest of the contents of your luggage.

———

Keep your travel bag stocked with all the travel-sized products you need and refill immediately once you get home. That way it's ready at a moment's notice.

———

When you're packing, roll your outfits together, or fold and place them in gallon-sized zip-top bags, so every outfit is ready to go. This makes unpacking and getting dressed while on vacation hassle-free.

———

Keep cords and chargers bundled in small bags when not in use or when traveling so they don't get tangled or dirty.

POCKET-SIZED TRAVEL KIT

If you're always on the go and like to be prepared, this hack is for you! Convert a breath mints container into a handy kit for items you may need while traveling, such as emergency sewing supplies, gum, and lip balm. This container fits nicely into a purse or pocket, so it's at your fingertips in case you need to quickly mend something or soothe chapped lips on the go.

WHAT YOU'LL NEED

Newspaper

1 (2⅓" × 3¾" × 1¼") rectangular metal mint container, such as an Altoids mint container, washed and dried

1 (12-ounce) can spray paint in a favorite color

1 (30') roll of washi tape

INSTRUCTIONS

1. Go outside and cover a surface with newspaper to protect from overspray. Open the tin and place it facedown on the newspaper. Spray paint it with three light, even coats until totally covered, with ten minutes drying time between coats. Make sure to cover every side except the interior; you'll want to keep that area free of paint so contents don't get contaminated. Let it dry completely before closing, around twenty-four hours.

2. Using washi tape, decorate the front of the container. You may wish to cover the entire front with washi tape by applying it in strips across the top from edge to edge or just do a few stripes if you like the paint color. Get creative!

3. Once you're finished decorating, fill it with your travel items and tuck it into a bag, glove compartment, or pocket when traveling.

If your favorite face cream doesn't come in a travel size, place it in a screw-top contact lens case for a mess-free way to tote small amounts of your favorite product.

———

When traveling, help prevent leaks in your personal care products that have screw-top lids by placing plastic wrap inside containers between the lid and the opening and screwing on the top to prevent spills.

———

Double up leak protection by making sure all bottles and tubes containing liquid are sealed in clear zip-top bags. Pack a few extra zip-top bags for the return journey just in case.

———

Inexpensive pop-up hampers are a great way to handle dirty laundry while on long trips. Fold it up and place the hamper in your luggage, then pop it up when you reach your destination as a collection spot for dirty clothes.

———

If you're traveling to a destination in which you intend to do a lot of shopping, pack an empty backpack or duffle in your luggage to carry home purchases.

Store small jewelry in plastic screw-top containers when traveling, such as medicine bottles or bead jars from the craft store. This keeps jewelry from getting tangled, and the hard sides protect the items as well.

———

When packing, keep night clothes and day clothes separate from each other. This makes unpacking upon arrival much less of a hassle, especially when it's late at night or you're dealing with travel delays. You can just pull out your pajamas and snooze!

———

If you have a favorite makeup remover or toner, wet cotton balls or cotton pads with the product and place them in a tightly sealed jar. This saves time and space by not having to bring along both the toner bottle and makeup remover pads.

PACKING WITH THE GRID SYSTEM

Anyone who has ever packed for vacation can attest to how easy it is to accidentally forget something. You don't want to be the one responsible for leaving behind a necessity like a bathing suit. The grid packing method solves that problem by easily arranging items according to the amount of days on the trip, the number of people, and what is needed. Once you learn how to grid pack, you'll never go back!

WHAT YOU'LL NEED

Large flat surface such as a bed

1 suitcase per person

Items to pack

INSTRUCTIONS

1. Count the number of people for whom you'll be packing. That's how many columns you will need. Put that person's suitcase at the top of each column to keep track.

2. Figure out what you need for each day. Each day gets a row. Add extra rows for items you'll use throughout the trip. For example, if you are packing for four days, you need four rows plus extra rows for items such as bathing suits and pajamas at the bottom.

3. Start placing items in the rows under the suitcases. When packing outfits, keep all of the clothes for each day together so it's easy to make sure you have everything you need.

4. Once finished, your flat surface will neatly be covered in items to pack. Simply collect the items under each person's suitcase and pack it. No more forgotten socks!

VEHICLES

Trash in the car is inevitable but it doesn't have to take over. Use a flip-top cereal holder or a reusable lunchbag with a flat bottom as handy trash containers while on the road.

Keep a car emergency kit in your trunk at all times. Stock it with a flashlight, hand sanitizer, a roll of toilet paper, ponchos, trash bag, paracord, and a first aid kit, and you'll be prepared for just about anything. Place everything in a handled container such as a toolbox in case you need to grab it and go.

Place silicone baking cups inside your car's cup holders for easy-to-clean spill protection.

Place a laundry basket in the trunk of your car when running errands. Use it to corral that day's items and then easily carry everything into your home.

COLLAPSIBLE CAR TRUNK ORGANIZER

Car trunks are often stuffed with reusable bags, items to return, groceries, emergency supplies, and general junk—all items that can completely overtake such a small space. This clever car trunk organizer not only solves that problem but also folds out when needed and stores flat when you don't.

WHAT YOU'LL NEED

2 hot glue sticks

Hot glue gun

3 (11" × 11" × 8") foldable storage cubes

1 pack medium-sized alphabet stickers

INSTRUCTIONS

1. Insert a hot glue stick into the hot glue gun and plug it in so it heats up, approximately five minutes. Arrange your cubes in a row with the sides touching and the folds facing front. If your cubes come with removable inserts, take those out.

2. Moving quickly yet carefully with the hot glue gun, cover the entire right side of the first cube and attach it to the left side of the next cube. Push together firmly for one minute to make sure the glue properly adheres to the cubes.

3. Cover the right side of the middle cube in glue, and then attach it to the left side of the third cube. Again, push firmly together for one minute until glue dries.

4. Label each bin using alphabet stickers, based on what you plan on using each bin for. Make sure to work around the folds and not apply stickers over them. Open up the cubes and replace bottom inserts. Now your organizer is ready to whip that car trunk into shape!

MOVING

· · · · · · · · · · · · ·

When packing moving boxes, fill them to the top so they don't get crushed but don't make them so heavy that it's a struggle to carry them. Pillows, light blankets, and comforters are perfect for filling those last few inches without adding much weight.

Beer and wine boxes with cardboard separators are awesome for packing glassware and fragile items for moving.

Never load important paperwork on the moving truck! You never know what you might need to have on hand when closing on a home or signing a lease. Keep those files with you whenever possible.

When moving, make sure that beds are the very first thing you set up. Then whenever exhaustion hits, the hard part is done and you'll have a place to nap or snooze.

Always use two strips of packing tape on the bottom of moving boxes to keep them safe from opening unexpectedly.

Make your toolbox the last thing you put on the truck and the first thing you unload. You're going to need it to reassemble furniture, break down boxes, or hang items on walls.

Create a "first day" kit in a laundry basket and fill it with needed items such as toilet paper, paper towels, and trash bags. Take this with you in the car when you move. This ensures you have all the necessities on hand and won't need to run to the store when you're already exhausted.

Organizing and unpacking your new kitchen can be confusing when you don't know where everything goes just yet. Solve this problem by writing out Post-it notes with categories of items, such as spices, pots and pans, dishes, and glassware, and placing them on cabinets and drawers. When you unpack, you'll have a plan and know exactly where to put things. It also helps you remember the location of items that first week in the house!

Label boxes with the room in which they need to go, and hang signs on those rooms for the movers. This is especially helpful with bedrooms, which are not always obvious.

10 THINGS TO GET RID OF RIGHT NOW

As you start packing for your move, you will want to clear out some of the refuse and junk that you won't want to bring with you to the new house. A surefire way to jump-start your organizing and decluttering is to do a massive clutter purge. If you want a list of common household items you can toss or recycle without agonizing over the decision, look no further:

1. Wire hangers (take to a dry cleaner for recycling)

2. Newspapers and magazines

3. Plastic shopping bags

4. Empty boxes

5. Expired food

6. Expired medicine

7. Expired coupons

8. Grocery store receipts

9. Beauty products you no longer use or are over twelve months old

10. Instruction manuals for products you no longer own

SEASONAL

· · · · · · · · · · · · · · · ·

Secure your keys onto a carabiner clip attached to the handle of your beach bag. Losing your keys in the sand would *not* be a fun way to end the perfect beach day.

———

If your crew is in the water all summer long, you'll find that having a drying rack in a handy spot is a lifesaver. As soon as you get home, drape towels and rinsed bathing suits on the rack (perhaps on the deck in the warm sunshine) so they're ready for the next splash down.

———

Use zip-top bags to store snacks in your beach bag so sand and moisture don't spoil the fun. Keep sunscreen and bug spray zipped in bags as well to prevent them from leaking and ruining clothing or towels.

———

Store pool and beach toys in mesh-sided bags so moisture and sand won't ruin your toys.

ORNAMENT STORAGE BOX

Protect precious ornaments and small holiday decorations in a hard-sided ornament storage bin that you can make yourself. With a few small tweaks, you can transform a bin you already own into specialized storage that saves you heartbreak from broken ornaments. The best part is that this project uses items you may already have on hand!

WHAT YOU'LL NEED

3 hot glue sticks

Hot glue gun

40 (9-ounce) clear plastic tumbler cups

2 (13" × 20") cardboard pieces

1 (58-quart) plastic storage tub with lid

Bubble wrap

INSTRUCTIONS

1. Insert a hot glue stick into the hot glue gun and plug it in so it heats up, approximately five minutes. Before gluing, place the cups on top of the first piece of cardboard in five rows of four cups each. Once the cups are in place and lined up, use the hot glue gun to apply glue to the bottom of each cup and adhere them to the cardboard by applying light pressure for a few seconds. Repeat this step with the second piece of cardboard and remaining cups, letting both dry for approximately five minutes.

2. Place the first piece of cardboard with the cups into the plastic tub. Fill each cup with an ornament. For especially fragile ornaments, you may wish to wrap them with bubble wrap before placing them into the cups for added protection. Once the bottom layer is filled, place the second cardboard/cup combination on top and fill those cups with ornaments. Fill any space on top between the cups and the lid with bubble wrap for added protection.

HOLIDAYS

Hooks along attic and basement walls are a great place to hang seasonal decorations such as plastic pumpkin pails, garlands, and wreaths when not in use. For wreaths, place in white trash bags, write the holiday on the outside with marker, and hang on hooks.

Wrap string lights around wrapping paper tubes for a tangle-free holiday experience. You can also wrap them around plastic hangers and hang them up in a closet until needed.

Fairy lights are smaller versions of string lights and can be rolled around empty paper towel tubes. Store rolls of fairy lights together in a plastic shoe box.

Place small ornaments in egg cartons to protect them and keep them from getting lost among the larger items.

Tinfoil and plastic wrap boxes are the perfect size for storing small ornaments and decorations. The rigid sides provide added protection, plus they can be lined up neatly inside your holiday bins.

Holiday decorations can be overwhelming. Start by sorting decorations by season. If you have an overabundance for one holiday, then sort and store in bins by category, such as ornaments, entertaining, lights, and wrapping supplies. Be sure to label the bins on the front, side, and top so you can find the correct ones from any direction you look.

Cardboard drink carriers from your favorite coffee shop are great for ornament storage. Line them on the bottom of a bin and place round ornaments in the indents where the cups would go.

Holiday photo cards are tough to toss because they contain photos of those you love. Instead, keep them in photo albums by year and pull them out each season. It's fun to look back on how everyone has grown over the years.

Have dedicated spots for your umbrellas, whether it's a hook in the garage or a place in your car or both. Once you get in the habit of always storing them in the same spots and grabbing them as needed, you won't be caught soaked in the rain again.

WAYS TO DISPOSE OF CLUTTER

Purging is one of the most important steps in organizing. As you organize, resolutely declutter each area with the mindset that less is more: Less junk means more room, more money in your pocket, and more room to breathe. You can make a little bit of money from your cast-offs by selling them piecemeal, or you can get rid of them in one fell swoop; the choice is yours, depending on your end goals. Here are ten places where you can dispose of your clutter and move forward with living happily in your newly organized space:

1. Sell items online on sites such as *Craigslist, eBay,* or local *Facebook* yard sale groups. This takes some time and often requires meeting up with strangers or dealing with shipping, so keep that in mind if you decide to go this route. Many police stations offer secure trading locations to keep you and your family safe.

2. Donate household goods and clothing to thrift stores or homeless shelters. Many charity organizations will come and pick up your donations for free. Find them online or watch for postcards that often get mailed a week or so before their truck comes to your neighborhood.

3. Schools, libraries, and hospitals are a few places that will welcome your gently used books.

4. Many churches and homeless shelters collect unopened personal care products to give those in need such as soap, shampoo, and toothpaste. This is a great place to donate unopened samples, hotel room freebies, and extra products gained from using coupons.

5. Stained or ripped clothing can often be reused if sent to organizations that repurpose them. Call thrift stores in your area or search online for local organizations to see if they accept clothing in subpar condition before you toss them.

6. Pet shelters need old towels, blankets, and newspapers and will usually welcome those donations with open arms.

7. Earn money on your nicer pieces by selling or consigning them in consignment shops. The protocol differs depending on the store, but often they will either pay you a flat price up front for your items or will consign them and pay you if the items sell. You can also search for online consignment stores that do the same thing; simply mail in your items and they send you a check.

8. Sell everything in one fell swoop at a big yard sale. At the end of the sale, donate all the leftovers to the thrift store or call a charity truck to come pick up the items. Don't hang on to the remaining items or you'll start back at square one!

9.   Set up a clothing swap with friends. Everyone brings items they don't want, and leaves with clothing that they do want. This also works for books and other items. It can be a fun way to get rid of the old and find something "new to you"; just make sure to leave with less than you came with if decluttering is your goal. Anything leftover is donated to charity, so it's win-win for all involved.

10. If you have too much stuff to deal with and not enough time, call a junk pickup service. You'll pay for them to haul away the load but there's something gratifying about having everything all gone at one time. Plus you won't have to haul it all away yourself.

US/METRIC CONVERSION CHART

VOLUME CONVERSIONS

US Volume Measure	Metric Equivalent
⅛ teaspoon	0.5 milliliter
¼ teaspoon	1 milliliter
½ teaspoon	2 milliliters
1 teaspoon	5 milliliters
½ tablespoon	7 milliliters
1 tablespoon (3 teaspoons)	15 milliliters
2 tablespoons (1 fluid ounce)	30 milliliters
¼ cup (4 tablespoons)	60 milliliters
⅓ cup	90 milliliters
½ cup (4 fluid ounces)	125 milliliters
⅔ cup	160 milliliters
¾ cup (6 fluid ounces)	180 milliliters
1 cup (16 tablespoons)	250 milliliters
1 pint (2 cups)	500 milliliters
1 quart (4 cups)	1 liter (about)

WEIGHT CONVERSIONS

US Weight Measure	Metric Equivalent
½ ounce	15 grams
1 ounce	30 grams
2 ounces	60 grams
3 ounces	85 grams
¼ pound (4 ounces)	115 grams
½ pound (8 ounces)	225 grams
¾ pound (12 ounces)	340 grams
1 pound (16 ounces)	454 grams

OVEN TEMPERATURE CONVERSIONS

Degrees Fahrenheit	Degrees Celsius
200 degrees F	95 degrees C
250 degrees F	120 degrees C
275 degrees F	135 degrees C
300 degrees F	150 degrees C
325 degrees F	160 degrees C
350 degrees F	180 degrees C
375 degrees F	190 degrees C
400 degrees F	205 degrees C
425 degrees F	220 degrees C
450 degrees F	230 degrees C

BAKING PAN SIZES

American	Metric
8 x 1½ inch round baking pan	20 x 4 cm cake tin
9 x 1½ inch round baking pan	23 x 3.5 cm cake tin
11 x 7 x 1½ inch baking pan	28 x 18 x 4 cm baking tin
13 x 9 x 2 inch baking pan	30 x 20 x 5 cm baking tin
2 quart rectangular baking dish	30 x 20 x 3 cm baking tin
15 x 10 x 2 inch baking pan	30 x 25 x 2 cm baking tin (Swiss roll tin)
9 inch pie plate	22 x 4 or 23 x 4 cm pie plate
7 or 8 inch springform pan	18 or 20 cm springform or loose bottom cake tin
9 x 5 x 3 inch loaf pan	23 x 13 x 7 cm or 2 lb narrow loaf or pâté tin
1½ quart casserole	1.5 liter casserole
2 quart casserole	2 liter casserole

INDEX

· · · · · · · · ·